Soul Repair thru

Art Therapy

The perfect handbook for teachers, counsellors and parents to ensure that their wards succeed and maintian a healthy equilibrium in their prosperous lives in this not-so-perfect world

By Pradeep Maheshwari

Academy of Behavioral Therapy

New Delhi

A word from the author.

All my life's learning and spiritual awareness are laid bare for you; every word is wrung out from my soul to pass on what I have managed to imbibe from an active and varied life. I hope my language is upto to this challenge. I think it will prove to be the perfect handbook for teachers, counsellors and parents to ensure that their wards succeed and maintian a healthy equilibrium in their prosperous lives in this not-so-perfect world. Subjects covered -

Pragmatic Psychology, Occult-spiritual psychology, Therapy & Counselling through Art.

Discussions on Suicide, Children, Consequences of Choices, the Power of words, Destiny & Fate, Success in the material world, and much more.

Contact: gururdeva@yahoo.com

phone India(0091) – 011 41730043

On Facebook look me up under PRADEEP PK MAHESHWARI & my group & page under the name: Academy of Behavioral Therapy

Person to person counseling and workshops offered·

Feel free to contact me anytime between 3-6pm

Book 1 Pragmatic Psychology

The Psychological Situation in this technological world.

The new life-styles that we are now sporting by the use of technical advancements has isolated our physical dependence on each other and as there is really no need to be there in person to communicate or create or work on a project, we now live bubble lives. The interchange of vital energies that occurs in personal face to face contact is now missing and we now live totally within our own vibes, whatever they are, without stress but also without any refreshing changes entering our atmosphere. There is a certain amount of morbid build-up. We are surrounded in major part by our own prepondent tendencies. This creates a vortex of self-indulgent vibes and pockets in our lives that can be not only limiting but also depressing and fatiguing to the Spirit.

It may be the information age but nobody is reading or bothering to inform oneself. Self-improvement although professed is the last thing on anybody's mind. Perseverance is weakening and tempers shortening. It is a sad age. There is much to read, easily available but lesser number of people than ever actually bother to make the effort to read – they are happy with the pictures and a few headlines and it is so much easier to lap up the ready-made concepts being dished out by the media. It is as if their growth has come to a stop and they are not interested in growing up further.

Well I am not here to change your world or even advising anything on those lines. Changes bring upheavals and that is definitely not practical or pragmatic or actually desired under these terms.

But yes, with little effort on the personal level, the vibes can be changed to reflect more positivity and openness – without diluting the personal content of our go-getting plans.

My prescription:

1)   A good friend to talk to

2) A good hobby like painting in oil. Or physical activity that requires focus such as table tennis or badminton.

How things will turn out at any given time is a big question mark and anxiety attacks are common. When hopes do not go to fruition as expected, there is depression in its wake.

Society t is not making things easy. The lack of humane feelings in today's professional attitudes is so unbelievable. And I am not talking of any specific people. Take anyone - a little power over you or your affairs and they misuse it to the full by leading you the honey-trap path.

Every error is capitalised upon. A little error and they take you to the cleaners. Take bankers, lawyers, policemen, doctors even the clerks in the municipal offices.
Every fault or small situation is taken with absolute seriousness and the problem is magnified to its full potential. You end up paying to get out of the predicament which out of sheer kindness and humaneness could have been overlooked with a warning.
It is demonic when the medical, military, policing people do it for gain as they who are Gods to us and we go to them in trust, yet they play with

our health, life and well-being fully knowing the horror that they are inflicting on us.

Parents, Teachers of children, Business bosses, and Successful businesses become arrogant about the power they wield and their self-importance goes right through the roof. Often it translates into careless hurtful behaviour because they know that they are protected by their position or seniority or often by law.

Marriages too are not immune to this effect.
But they take refuge in laws, rules and procedures. And we have no protection against this. What gives these people such stone-hard hearts?

We are quite really to blame for the spots we get into. To be happy not much is required. But then our desires never stop sprouting. If only we would focus more on the wishes that have been fulfilled and aspire for more but without agitation.

The healing practices and the policing style of a people give their characters away. Some treat life as if at war.

In India today if we take this as a guideline, then we would look to be - Unfair, Self-profiting, callous, cheats and at the same time kind and helpful but not able to work together.

From the trainer's point of view, I have seen all training remain a superficial activity as the base nature finally predominates.

There is another method too. Forge alliances. Nourish each other. Grow and flourish. In healing this would be: Care, Compassion, Learning, Self-control, Preventive methods + respect for the body as an entity.

Our thinking of lack of respect to life even shows in the healing sciences as practised in the modern systems. Some of the modern treatments make me think of medieval warfare: Attack castle – breach the wall – burn – leave no place for people to hide – rape and kill and enslave the rest. After total devastation, come home and call it a great victory. Just check on how they treat "cancer" and you will understand the mind-set I am trying to describe.

And they actually use the word "battle" for it.

Our greatest efforts go into contradicting. Nothing particular is aimed at. Simply we find it difficult to accept that anyone else be seen in a better light than us.

The lower the Emotional quotient and intellectual broadening of the mind, the greater is the effort to first contradict and think later.

Why does our envy raise its head whenever we find somebody else saying something worth appreciating? Or doing something so well that it is praise all around? And admittedly better than us!

It is so sad to see people being childishly churlish by looking for faults, errors and even countering with exaggerated personal comments to somehow show another in poor light.

I have seen often that comments bubble up in the listener/reader even before the other person has finished saying or whatever he is saying has even registered.

A good game that these people play is by picking on a word or phrase and then going at tangent in a totally unconnected stream and thereby confusing the issue intentionally; putting the other guy in a position to explain and defend his point.

How does one deal with this?

- By not falling into the trap of argument. Just keep your peace and respond with silence or/and a smile, this puts them off no end. Leave them to their devices. And if it is bosses, just make sure by documentary or other evidence that you made your point and that you are not responsible for the decisions.

In personal relations I, often reply with – "I have said what I had to say. You can make whatever you want of it" and in other places like with my wife, I do not even try to make a suggestion…… until absolutely crucially necessary.

Growing up is a process few are aware of.

Most of us connect growing up with the wrinkles on our faces and the shape of our figure. Little or no effort is put into the growth of the persona and learning to go beyond one's own self. Rather all the effort is put in NOT growing up. One wants to remain at a perpetual 20-30 age level.

The effort to stop ageing is the focal point which then becomes such a childish pursuit.

Do you know anyone closely who carry "Resentment" as a crown?

They give the impression that there is no way that the world can ever please them. The commas and semi-colons are always out of place. Their need to put things to right is perennial. They feel superior and even sad by the world's need imposed on them to keep things in order. The impression they give is that it is their forced duty to be harsh on the world - not that they enjoy it.

But if you ask me they enjoy it supremely. And they maintain this facade because it is so satisfying to see others grovel to keep them in good humour.

My personal observation is that eventually these people lose the most as they end up alienating everybody and as they advance in years, the need for support increases and the opposite starts happening around them.

Some people are really lucky. They have limited needs, simple minds and they don't suffer with vivid imaginations to bother them with fear and possibilities – good and bad. They always have more than they need and they are quite happy to be left alone to their devices. Their good luck gives them a good job in which they excel because they have no ulterior motives and not much ambition either to compete. Or life provides them in other ways.

It is a life that is full with preoccupations of making the bed and washing the clothes.

This is the reason why their personal relations are at a minimum and they would rather not have people in their lives; yet they are intelligent enough to know that they need others but it is an ongoing battle with their personal world and the world at large.

It is sad to see these people because they allow themselves to be trapped in a limited world in which there is no entry for strangers. They have no need to improve on anything in this particular personalised world and least of all themselves. It is a lovely comfortable life in which they are content, happy at rearranging furniture instead of worrying about interior design and the next castle they will own.

I have met many of these kinds – even have had to live with them. The first thing I noticed was their ability to ignore all inputs from the world at large. They would simply ignore; this tendency also affecting how they dealt with their health. They refuse to listen to their bodies and tend to permit illness to fester to a point of pain before acting on it; which a conscious person would agree is already too late.

They suffer for it but do not wish to see the connection that their illness may have with their attitude. It is a blissful life until the avalanche hits them –and I have seen this happens in older age when the body can't take the abuse any more. At this point they fall into depressions or suffer from rages which alienate them even more from the world of friends and well wishers and unfortunately also from their own little world that they have created so arduously.

These people have such strong minds that some of us simpletons would be awed. They are good at making accusations, weaving logic with their wishes so elegantly that virtually everyone feels left out as the more worldly types see existence from other angles. The result is that you either listen to them or shut up. They can argue on till kingdom come. You have to finally give up in exasperation. Suggestions in their world become criticisms and even a hint of it can be the start of a "reaction".

My way has been to leave them alone, go along with them if I have to but emotionally, mentally, if not physically, keep a distance. Something that they enforce literally anyway; yet deep somewhere these souls are lonely and they so wish to be admired and be friends with the world; it is like a sad movie that you can see but not get involved.

The torment is real.

They want to be accepted as they are but life unfortunately is as unforgiving as they are.

The complex world and we.

Most of us aren't really that well in tune with the Cosmos. We are using largely a very tiny portion of our faculties in a huge world of great variety. The world is complex and most often there are influences at work that we do not understand, rarely even know about and we end up miscalculating our moves. In simple words we can say that we are buffeted by our simple desires and wishes and the problem is that so is everybody else. This results in clashes of wills and destinies. Millions of people living together but alone individually.

The instrument we use to get along is the mind and I feel it could use more input than it usually has to circumnavigate this sea of Creation. The question begs to be asked as to how some of us are successful and content while most of us in deep despair and disappointment although we may not show it; anyway, no one cares and we are wise enough to understand that our lives are not important to others unless we are of use or of some immediate profit to them. Largely speaking much of the world is already organised and we can bumble along in it quite comfortably. Society has been organised, laws of behaviour laid down, products and services designed and made for us – all that we need is some talent to earn a living and we can take care of most of our needs.
But the question is - Is that all? NO! We want so much more. Yet few seem to really make an effort to do so. And this is the crux of it all. Our

wishes are not commensurate with our readiness and preparation. I can safely say that we have been educated and inculcated with a not-so-correct know-how of this world at large and we have been actually prepared for depression and stress and not the other way round.

To live in this world requires a kind of enlightenment too.

We need to learn and know well:

- The human-made laws

- The psychology of humanity

- The education system

- Laws of physics, chemistry and biology at work

- Logic behind gadgetry and applications

- Know some carpentry. Plumbing and electricals

- When to speak and when to lie low/silent

- Naturopathy and how to maintain health

- How others will & can hurt us.

- The policing system

- The punishment system

- The monetary system

On what words were you brought up?

What words are you carrying in your subconscious? These words form the base of your persona. Everything you think and do is colored by these words.

Have you ever thought how your decisions are modulated by the words that you carry within?

It is now a well accepted fact that our personas are like icebergs. The greater, major part is submerged and remains unseen and yet upholds the little portion that is visible to the world. Every image that we carry since our day of birth is connected with words that went with the images. We interact with the world based on these images imprinted in our memory unknowingly and subconsciously.

Every world carries a little world in itself. It paints pictures in our minds and unleashes emotions in our hearts. So it goes without saying that we should be vary of the words we are bringing up our children on. And we should deeply meditate and focus on the words that we unleash from our mouth and the words that form part of our regular vocabulary. What words and phrases do you use most of the time?

Here is a small example:

A cyclist skids and falls down. These are the comments from passers-by:

- Are you hurt?
- Careless bugger.
- Watch where you are going.
- He wasn't paying attention.
- Hardly the age to go cycling.
- He had it coming to him.

You see from above what thoughts got motivated and what words were uttered it is not difficult to understand the state of mind of each commentator – people who care and who couldn't care less or are just happy to advise and criticise. Why? Because that is how they were made to think when growing up. This is what they heard and saw around them and their subconscious is replicating automatically.

Over 2,500 years ago, philosopher and poet Lao Tzu taught that our words become actions, which eventually become our destiny.

Subliminal Conditioning

The last century after the Great War, saw relatively a period of technical growth and a unified market at peace. So all countries could manufacture goods and sell in a larger market that had existed ever before. The wars had devastated large populations and there was great hunger for more. This is when with the reach now available to the media, also was growing thru unheard of mediums of travel by air, television and color photography and printing. There was a great jump in the people who could read and earn well. So there were buyers.
The marketers immediately saw the potential that was opening up. They centered and focused on sex but couched it in the word LOVE. This is how they made the people see things: to win over "love", give gifts, make yourself smart and presentable – this translated into gifts, clothes, cosmetics, dine-outs picnics and all things needed to show-off. This would then result in marriages; which in turn gave rise to more sales for the homes, and when the babies came along, it was bonanza for the sellers. It was an unending stream of buyers and a long list of desires waiting and

begging to be satisfied. Everyone had to have a car!

The aspirations grew but unfortunately most of us are not made for this competitive life and keep up with the Joneses. Envy, rancor became rampant. Individuality, independence & unrestrained freedom was aimed for and aloneness was wanted but at the same time so was "love" - a kind of living in a group without wanting to be part of it.

Imagine everyone living precariously on the edge of self-centeredness but depending on each other, knowing well that they need each other but not wanting to acknowledge this fact. A potent brew to bring pain in one's life is as I see it.

Is it a wonder that disturbed souls are now the norm rather than exceptions?

The media was becoming more and more refined with better and cheaper gadgetry and dreaming up more and more occasions for happiness. The reach was growing and the middle class was ecstatic with its possessions.

They were being bombarded from all sides, specially the movies and the stars to adopt more classy styles of living. The trap was well laid and the whole world fell into it with a thud – never realizing that they had been subliminally manipulated into this state.

This gave rise to stresses, poorer health, broken dreams and disappointments and psychotic break-downs. We literally sold our souls and paid for it like we were giving out dowry for the pleasure. This mess now demands clearing up.

Parenting is the source of most problems.

Lately in the past two years there have been many reports of "honour" murders where parents or brothers murder their own. What message is this giving to other children and about the society we are living in; when we are so convinced that we are doing the right thing - even murder is acceptable?

There is definitely a case for bad conditioning in the way the younger people in "too-free" societies are evolving. All the film stories in vivid color, games and programs on TV tend towards self and egoistic satisfaction with violence if needed.

Children are just happening. That is the tragedy. There is no real wanting for a child to cherish and bring up properly most of the time.

We talk of their rights and we pose in our virtuousness, showing off how much value we give to each life. But do we really?

I have been advocating this idea since many years:

1) No kids till you have the means; an income and education.

2) Pre training for marriage and kids - six months course. This will give them time to reconsider too.

3) No divorce if you have kids. Suffer for your pleasure and parents to get jail terms too for their kids.

I say: Have your sexual escapades but once you have a child, you need to forget yourself and devote yourself to the child's welfare totally to the best of your ability.

And then, don't have a child unless you have the establishment that can give a good home, education and guarantee unstinted love and security to the child

In today's heavily populated world, there is also a logistic problem. The point is that too many children ruin more families than make them. And we end up having vagabonds. Giving an education is not a joke. And semi literate person like the masses are beginning to be is of no help. Our schools are full but that's about it. There are no teachers of caliber – no real infrastructure and no exposure to the world at large. The atmosphere in the families is not conducive to study.

And finally there are no jobs for the adults now and don't see much improvement in the future. Our technological world requires education.

My philosophy has always been: the child comes first. And we need to consciously work and plan projects to give the children as much exposure to life as possible but this requires time and money and a great will. So, fewer children will get better results.

This is something quite rare and life on earth will change when this happens commonly. Most parents put themselves first – their individual bents and desires, their career, business, social life etc and the neglect the child feels goes beyond calculation. This is a fact in my eyes although I have yet to meet anyone who agrees. The joint-family and open communities were such a boon in earlier days

We give birth to children and then leave them to grow up on their own with little or no guidance worth the name. They grow up picking up influences from their surroundings without ever learning discernment and self-control.

The personas are not being helped to mature beyond this point. Much of the blame for misery is directly connected to the vibrations and acts we are letting happen through us.

Then, we believe, that the soul chooses what misfortune it wants to face. So often unexplained misery visits which is seen as tragedy.

Easy words. But how many of us given time to contemplating what exactly constitutes the elements that makes us. Do we remember the children we were?. That was the original.

In materialistic cultures, physical pleasures are on top of the list. Sex is the highest joy known and understood. Eating for pleasure is the second. Speed and fearsome activities like racing and mountaineering are others. But finding a sexual partner seems to be the highest goal - new ones every now and then add to heighten the pleasure. The stupendous amount of energy that is spent in pursuing an insatiable & exhausting goal and at the same time the complications that we create for ourselves is mind boggling.

Earlier there was a concerted attempt to teach and train kids for life. But now we have metamorphosed into a material culture where goods and the ready-money at one's disposal makes a "man"; too early, too much can only end up being misused and result in confusion, hurt and pain.

Parents can become ogres sometimes. The tendency is to treat children as possessions to do as they please which can often translate into dictatorial and highly punishment oriented characters.

The entire enigma of existence is hidden behind the fact that every individual is totally certain that he has "seen" the world, knows all there is to really know and is perfectly attuned to understanding each and every other person and phenomena.

If the above assumption be true then of course there is nothing that can be taught to this person nor is he in a frame of mind to learn. And as a corollary it is easy to understand why he will never understand a new point of view and all attitudes not to his way of thinking automatically become non-relevant and suspect.

In most cases this can be seen to be the root cause behind our tendency to see others as silly & not in the know. Our arrogance then takes the onerous job of correcting and teaching the wayward thinker the standardized truth.

Let them be. Really; let them be. Just do not get pulled into their vortex. Don't become them but don't treat their lives as questionable either. If you have to be with them, BE. Just be and nothing more. It is their planet and we are guests. Live like guests. No faulting and comparing with our "Higher & Better principles". No uppity thoughts to mar the pleasure of the situation. Simply ride the waves and be cool within. Don't get unnerved, don't be critical; just make the best of it – happy to have their company.

There is an imperative need to stand out; vanity insists. But it is shadowed by an imperative fear of being alienated from the crowd.

Between the two we die a slow certain death with stress as our constant companion.

Yes. I see whole lives spent in policing others. Looking for faults and getting irritated and irritating others. Just so any focus from oneself can be avoided. And then feel superior as well.

Reading the Soul

To be able to care for another and nurse a certain level of sensitivity to the other person's vibes is required. There cannot be and there is not a codified rigid method to go by although psychiatrists do try to do so. But even for ordinary mortals who find it difficult to read others, two things come in good stead and will be greatly helpful: compassion & deep listening. All that is really required is that we become relatively quiet and let the other person tell his story and believe the other person's version totally without any critical thoughts from our own side.

And if we could learn to see into the destinies of our students then we could really help by supporting the other person without becoming a permanent pillar and crutch. This always proves of great help – being there, giving moral support and helping the student to unravel his own state of mind. Astrology, numerology, palmistry and such exotic sciences have been used to see into the destined wavelengths of others since thousands of years. I personally feel that they do help.

I have been studying numerology since the age of 17. I find the Chaldean system of numerology as practised, perfected and shown in the book by Cheiro " Cheiro's Book of Numbers" is very accurate... I have 50 years of personal experience of using it has never lead me astray. I can safely say that it gave me the insight into individuals and situations and helped me decide how far to go and where not to waste my energies. Certain situations demand help and should be helped out; all they need is a little push but then there are others that are best left alone as they are not ready for change and often the whole affair can backfire on you.

Therapeutically Counselling thru Art.

The Science of Self rediscovery through Art Therapy leading to a deeper understanding to the solutions to disturbed mind-states and their causes. Helping others realize their full potential through ART by making their art a reflection of their own persona and thereby assist them to discover equilibrium in life and the truth of their own being.

The concept of Art Therapy.

The word Therapy implies that something is out of order. That something in the human persona needs to be put right vis-à-vis the pragmatic realities of life. It presupposes that the person in front of us is in a state of disturbance and that assistance to recreate a balance and equilibrium is required. Yes; this is quite what happens. Life is a distinctly awful mix of love, kindness, sacrifice at one end and dislike, jealousy and disdain at the other. Often for no reason other than selfish interest it gets even worse - Dislike turns to hate and venomous thoughts and actions take shape. Opportunities are difficult to come by and when we do not know what to do, despair takes over. But then I am not here to discuss basic psychology. The point is that these elements enter the life of a person from the day he is born. In many traditions, it is believed and even science today is now accepting it that the influences begin even before birth.

It is this push and pull of society and the way the world is running that creates dissonance in individuals who have either not been brought up properly or educated properly or readied for the life ahead properly. We

21

can't blame anybody but we must yet try and understand the factors at play. Therapy can help by mainly being a good listener and imparting and sharing of knowledge of the world so that the disturbed person can reorient himself and find the supportive pole to support his life. All that a desperate intellect is looking for is answer to tough questions. The healer can help by listening after ascertaining their sincerity or comment on pragmatic matters and let it be. The job of thinkers is to make people think, specially for their selves for their betterment – and this they will do only when they desire it and that point comes only when they are tired of it all and ready to take the plunge towards something new.

Taking the role of a therapist is a big responsibility. You may end up supporting more than you had bargained for.

What is art therapy?

When the mind gets too focused on one goal to the exclusion of all else, there is a tightening which results in knots in the mind that become habits in the long run. This creates a pattern of thinking and action that is self-defeating with the individual not even aware of it + past memories create a lot of logjam. We need to break away from them. Let the past recede far enough so that new impressions can make a home in our personalities.

We cannot always change our patterns but by changing some of our activities we can create new paths in our brain's way of handling things. Try Painting in Oil. This is a wonderful medium to take your mind off on a tangent. By using forms and colors, a door is opened to new vistas.

Even depression can be reined in. Therapists force the clients to paint pictures of happy things or scenes such as flowers and landscapes with a lot of yellow and green in them. This is in contrast to gloomy moods where most people tend towards black or very dark, heavy colors and forms. Not only primary colors. Let's not limit ourselves and take a rigid stance. The colors that are vibrant are yellows and every shade of every color in which it is to be found. White too. It is simply impossible to be unhappy with these colors in your lives. Left to themselves, most humans would go on masturbating with their own morbid thoughts. So they have to be weaned away. The ego of a person will resist so the job has to be done gently. Landscapes with pleasant forms and all elemental natural ingredients in it are just the thing to help deflect, reflect & reset our orientation of thoughts.

To be a good therapist you have to be a good listener and very empathetic.

Today the disturbed people have a valid reason to be so. They are dispossessed by kings in such a way that the hunger pangs leave no time or alternative but to look elsewhere. Then the TV has opened their eyes to easier possibilities "ready-made" solutions. The temptation is too great and between their desires and short-cuts they get totally lost.

It is the time element. They are too much in a hurry. Everyone wants their share of enjoyment "now". At the back of their minds is the thought that can always snatch it from others if nothing else and the means are seemingly available to all.

Knowledge is available in plenty. There is even the state of overload now. The problem is of whom to give it to. Everyone's cup is full with all that they really require.

The superficial, slothful & self-satisfied humanity is busy with inanities.

The human mind is like absorbent cotton. IT has many redeeming features which it never uses. For instance it has an intelligent feature wherein it can analyse and shut off unwanted influences (like and anti-virus program in the computer) but it rarely is used - it allows all inputs to go into the subconscious and then react to it. The memory is never used as a learning tool to remember and not repeat history. No effort is made by the conscious mind to stop its desire self and hurt the body and life around it. etc etc

The commercial world learnt this early in the last century when Freud and Jung made many things clear to the western world's commercial appetite. The consumer goods industry and the medical fraternity have made hay on this knowledge.

It had become obvious with the coming of the movies. But nobody would listen and still does not listen. The TV made it worse. Now the smart phone has totally taken over. Coca cola and party has done the rest.

Communications in today's world has reached a level of unprecedented deafness. The tendency of old habits is to avoid making a change and delay it as much as possible. When it comes to "cliché" behaviour, have you observed how systemised some people can be?. Why has our culture remained stagnant? Because we are not ready to part or come out of the accepted comfort zone - we have imposed upon us a fixed "syllabi" of life and not prepared to look further.

It is so funny to hear people voicing hundreds of years old clichés as they are the first ones to have said it. Our stories are the same and in the name of tradition we continue doing the same things as if it was the first time and an innovation we have just thought of. And of course everyone cheers wildly.

Just see the story-lines, style of acting of our films and you will understand what I am saying. Pick one average film from each year since 1950 and you will see the "formula" embedded.

The life-job for each of us is to reach in this life the highest level of positive and compassionate consciousness we can and help others with our experience of the way without interfering in the destiny or lives of others. The moment it becomes anything more, it will suck. Never forget: giving advice is one thing; taking decisions for others without full understanding of the "destiny" at work can be bad for us and others.

What would really be a good lesson is sharing of our personal experiences from our growth stories – how we climbed one step higher on the ladder of self-improvement; if we have the courage to do - and how we felt after the experience.

Examples of some photos/paintings and their analysis.

1) A very matured, Chinese type of painting from a 4 year old. Defies description. To me it seems indicative of acute sharpness in thinking. Clear-cut and brilliant.

26

2) A great photo from a 5 year old. The instinctive understanding of form and light is fabulous. Shows deep sensitivity to surroundings and ability to be one with it.

3) Another study. One can gauge the balanced personality behind this shot. Nothing excessive; simple and beautiful – complete in itself.

4) A lovely abstract from a happy well adjusted person.

5) In this the artist, a child, has seen a vision.

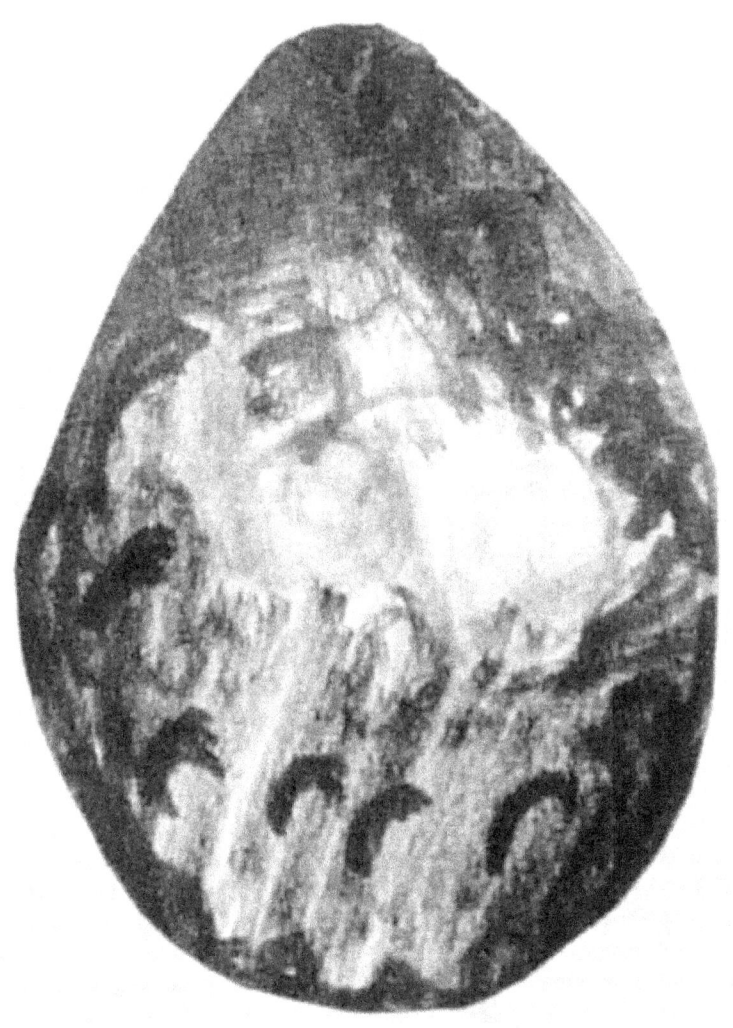

The "psychology" aspect of therapy.

True, we should be compassionate and caring. But often in life the best thing to do is to let others go their way and do what they will, without taking it personally or interfering in the name of help, and if they suffer for it, so be it.

A deeper understanding of the psychology and spiritual influences involved will go a long way to help you be a successful therapist. Here I give a collection of quotes and notes from my other conversations:

Please do not assume that because I am writing about something, it must be personal. Of course, it would certainly be part of an experience in my life and a lesson learnt – no doubt of that. But often I personalize it in a story –normally as a little comic - to make it easy for my listener to relate to. That is all. The joy, the pain and the experience is real but not always the short story made around it.

There is indolence, inertia and mental laziness in the human make-up. There is also arrogance and pride. We are also endowed with intelligence but we prefer to rely more on our pride. We take paths for which we are not ready and get into troublesome spots. We first are too lazy to prepare ourselves and later too weak to look for the objective solution. Situations go out of hand because we just don't have the required knowledge and understanding to deal with it. The better answer is in agreeing for change and actively pursuing it by going with the flow and learning as fast as we can as much as we can as the moment permits.

Humans judge by their minds which are under slavery to their petty wishes. The Cosmos has a different way of looking at things besides the human view of what is humane, good or nice. Some people are bigger than the pot that they try to stuff themselves in. Luckily destiny has other plans and keeps breaking the pot. In the experience of life after life, the problem and situation continues to pursue the individual till he rises above it.

Everyone wants help with their lives from others; their greatness demands it and they know that they deserve it. But when it comes to helping back, they have such pressing things in hand and on their mind that they feel surely it is of no importance. The lack of gratitude in our natures is greatly responsible for the lacks in our lives.

Pretensions to be good and virtuous are another bane. We pretend to be good, grateful, gracious& generous but never meaning it. We pretend to be spiritual by showing off our visits to temples and giving alms to beggars and what not. Inanities; all of this energy being spent on stuff that really is just gossip and good for whiling away time. Let us focus on the teachings and put them into practice. What is of importance is the experience onward and this we should be ready to share.

Let us not become collectors of data.

People are looking for information. They are collectors. The collection makes them feel rich. They have a quote for every occasion and they can rationalise and explain everything away. Change is not what they are looking for.

We are too much in a hurry to digest max from life - and then die of indigestion

We are brought up on too many prejudices and rules. This is stifling. We as therapists and people must grow out of it we are to find any kind of contentment. I found this poster on Facebook and show it to you here because it gives a good list of things we need to keep in mind.

12 Symptoms of Spiritual Awakening

1. An increased tendency to let things happen rather than make them happen.
2. Frequent attacks of smiling.
3. Feelings of being connected with others and nature.
4. Frequent overwhelming episodes of appreciation.
5. A tendency to think and act spontaneously rather than from fears based on past experience.
6. An unmistakable ability to enjoy each moment.
7. A loss of ability to worry.
8. A loss of interest in conflict.
9. A loss of interest in interpreting the actions of others.
10. A loss of interest in judging others.
11. A loss of interest in judging self.
12. Gaining the ability to love without expecting anything.

Then there is beauty in general to be considered. Keeping things pretty is why elaborate dresses are worn and this is where good taste comes in. Of course, there is the question of what is good taste and it can be very subjective. Very few of us are able to be objective and this where quarrels and dislikes begin. Yet, certain common factors have been prevalent and accepted by all in general over civilizations after civilisations - so they can be accepted as objective against the subjective.

\# The "ringer" of the telephone has more hold over our lives than life itself.

How did we come to this pass?

The smart phone is the ultimate instrument of slavery.

And let us not blame the messenger. The message behind it all is us:

Our need to let them know is so based on our need to make sure that they are remembering us. Then there is also our hidden need to be seen as someone special that we consider ourselves to be.

Situations happen to us because the time has come for us to weather them - and then be promoted to the next class. The lesson is never learnt in one go..... and we believe in continuation of the process into many lives, on and on till it is learnt; eventually they do.

Most distressful situations happen when the Soul wants to go in one direction, and the mind (desire mind) wants to go in another.

The knowledge of the forces behind life goes back many eons and there is nothing much to discuss there as it has been proven to be quite true by everyone who has taken this path.

Once, many many years ago, I was visiting Calcutta and picnicking on the lawns in the evening at the Victoria Memorial garden, a child from another family nearby came and sat on my lap. Just simply sat. No talk; as if he belonged there since ever. And quietly kept on sitting there. It was an ethereal moment. Then it was time for us to go. The child calmly stood

up and started walking with me. He wouldn't go back to his family.

I felt a huge lump in my throat and felt as something was tearing away when I had to forcefully let the child be taken by his parents.

The incident still haunts me. What connection was made and broken that day?

Where do I belong? With whom should I really be? Are there connections that were never made that are, though, to happen?

What do we really know of our destiny? What do we really understand about our relationships?

We are constantly in denial.

We deny the facts to ourselves and we find explanations to ignore them.

Misfortunes and other nefarious things happen to others- the state of illusion is astonishing.

Fate is derided.

Destiny is blamed.

Friends who dare to pin-point defects are disliked.

Doctors are branded charlatans.

Critics are monsters.

Everything is perfectly fine with "our" world!

Be compassionate with yourself. Step out of mental mind games and head chatter to find stillness within.

Life is what it is.

Every moment it tempts you with a lovely smelling, pretty flower.

Unknowingly you are being led by the nose.

You make of it what you will.

For the layman the approach of not doing because it is fate or karma that will do everything is negative because it gives them a socially acceptable excuse to do nothing and yet remain productive within the limits of society. It may keep them calm but in the final analysis it is a negative trend. This is the reason why sloth and refusal to embrace anything dynamic has become the main psychological tendency of India.

The world is in an evolution mode all the time - slowly at Mother Nature's speed. That is also true. But if we are to take this attitude of everything is perfectly fine as a lot of teachers are propounding with quotes like: You are Divine, You are perfect, Love yourself as you are……. then why even bother about talking about zen, yog, calm, meditation or anything?

For the yogi, on the path, of course, impatience would be a negative thing – even disastrous.

But for the average guy who really wants to change, there has to be "doing" even the state of getting started - the first step has to be taken -

this has to come from the will and then the mind has to be directed to follow a path with determination.

90% of the facts, accepted as truth, are erroneous (study history of accepted facts and you will see the joke) - more so from the occult perspectives. Just enjoy the joke this life is. And play along. If you analyse people's lives/thinking - the rights and the wrongs, you'll go mad.

There is much wisdom in being a little laid-back, keeping an hawk's eye on our mental arrogance. Laissez-faire is in order.

Changes come to people who have some element of sincerity already in their make-up. The cheaters learn their lessons only when cornered and beaten up and ostracised - till then their confidence and acts become more and more flagrant.

The problem with humor is that everyone's idea of humor is different & dependent on his/her level of consciousness and emancipation.

All people are not nice. Rather it is my experience that finding a real nice guy without an ulterior motive is a rarity. There are many people who are really bad. So be warned. There ARE people with strong vital personas and they can over-ride the mental processes of most weakling minds – minds that are childishly open to suggestions and have not learnt to stand by their own principles and do not use their will to stand their ground. These ungoverned minds actually collaborate in the process.

Sometimes it is difficult to create a shield against the avarice of manipulators but we can always run away from them for our own peace of mind.

As I understand - The energy here is of "Beings" that work using people as their conduit vessels.(one has to first accept that there are beings influencing occultly the affairs of men)

Yes - finally the cause or the major part of the situation can be traced to us - if we look into it sincerely.

Yes. To people who want to be strict, correctional and lecturing all the time. Please just be there for your child or friend, husband or wife. They can grow only at their pace. Be involved and involve them in your life fully. Play with your child and teach them everything you know thru play. Even small inconsequential things. Things that we take for granted but the children will know only if we tell them. This is the secret to be happy for ever and in better health than most.

The most nourishing food is that which is made with love and joy in one's heart.

Show me a rich man who became rich thru honest endeavor.

In the world as it is, integrity towards sincerity will always end up in lack of money although you may be rich spiritually

Exposure is the first step to change.

How exposed do you feel?

Will you in all sincerity permit exposure?

Can you stand the glare of spot-lights?

Why am I so afraid to let the Universe run things for me?

Why am I always interfering and bringing misery to myself?

Yoga is a way of life/attitude and philosophy. It is not something done separately like playing hockey. This is the error in promoting it as an addendum. The buyers of the charade are as much to blame as the greedy sellers.

Until humans get a hang of the working of their minds, they are going to remain as they are.

These people are not really, deeply interested in changing their habits and routines and study for their own benefit is not on their agenda. Everything is superfluous. They easily convince themselves that all foods and activities they are indulging in are already perfectly alright.

The mind is good at playing tricks on our understanding. You will meet a lot of people who take a virtuous stand by reducing some food elements like sugar or not eating at McDonald's. They feel they have done their part for their good health without ever paying attention to their general diet habits.

Similarly the same can be seen in other activities of life too.

And exercise? Where is the time for that? + They are convinced that all the household chores and the walking from their car to their office will be enough.

It's stronger than them. Technology now gives us the opportunity to stay cocooned in our own little un-evolved world.

Can you withdraw into yourself and just look without reacting?

The upper class will never let go.

They let things happen that are politically correct at the mass level.

Just because most them never speak out their private thoughts and intentions in public doesn't mean a thing.

How do I know?

Because even in my own heart, I have difficulty in accepting whatever is uncouth and feel that the masses are not learning from the opportunities that they have now - but in reverse roles they are imposing their mass standards on us.

What I call - we have brought the villages to town and are now overwhelmed by it.

Yet: The power is always in the hands of The Samurai and The Banker. Never the masses - yes - they do have a nuisance value.

A new study out of the US has revealed being married can make people more prone to depression, because constant nagging triggers deep-rooted stress.

Dr PK: very normal - the reality of marriage (made in heaven- my foot!)

Naggers use the technique of taking everything personally; it permits them to feel important and being offended is a part of it.

People come and go out of our lives. The act of jumping to conclusions and parting in a huff is so normal without giving the other a chance to explain. We can only continue on with our lives. - that is unless our egos are hurt!

Banning guns or anything or trying to stop human nature with legislation.

It's like blaming the messenger. The best defense has always been deterrent. Banning anything is shortsightedness but making it too easy to obtain everything is also not really good. It can and does also give ideas to otherwise calm people.

Then our shows of every kind are giving ideas to those who would have otherwise never thought of it. We show nefarious activities in such details, that it gives confidence to less evolved humans to enact the same.

It is not only guns; all the products that have been made available in plenty (often on credit) like alcohol, trans-fats, fast cars, cigarettes, sleeping pills, smart phones, to name a few, - have you any idea how many deaths occur due to them? This is without taking into account how we are hurting ourselves and others in the long term.

The reality is that all the factors are in play. It is finally the psyche of the man. Some elements are more pronounced in some areas than others.

Mentioning isolated events prove nothing. Let's focus on the illogical side of humanity. The rest are just incidences.

Unfortunately, and I have spoken on this many times before here, women gave away their power for homes. The vanity of having a man under their command, thru his addiction to sex and good cooking was more than enough for them + the reflected glory and social position that marriage brought them.

Nothing will change until the woman becomes the "man" again and subverts the "physical" childishness of the male to help them evolve beyond chimpazeeism..

Caste-ism, racism, fear of the unknown culture, self-protection is flowing in human blood as distilled stupidity.

I believe the best is to take the wind out of the sail of others is to take the joke on one self.

For instance I always take the joke on me like: - I am a poor failed guy, what do I have? - I am a failed uneducated guy who never went beyond class 4, what do I know?

There is this funny idea going around that you can eat as much as you want and then just go for a walk to sweat off your sins. Exercise can tone your metabolism but will not remove the extra filling-up.

Yes – simple: Everything is doable when we want to.

Humans look for excuses for their nefarious plans and books with religious backing have always been a good source. And there are many

such books. Looks more like the work of the devil to me. The morals are forgotten and the incidents remembered and obtain justification. In India I find the epics, Mahabharata and Ramayana have done more harm than good. Yet the main characters are now our greatest gods.

It's the spiritual leaders that ignite fires in the masses with ill intentioned interpretations.

Finally it is life that will win. And if we don't wish to perish, we will have to give it priority. In truth there is no problem... only relentless cussedness and we can or not join in the play.

You can't teach people who have been conditioned to be obedient. The effort to think is too much for some and others have their brains atrophied by the time they are 8. And if you can't teach, where will the teachers come from?

There is no beginning or end and you know that. As for depression, best stay away from it. It is always a case of overblown self-pity.

Then there is also the Indian way of continuously bringing the past up to put you on the back-foot before you can even speak forth about your present. Raking up the old is a good way to avoid the future.

We see what we see - as far as our eyes take us. Mine eyes only for me and thine for thee.

A string of words between us.

The world thinks there is a choice. Not really. We have situations and a "yes-no" choice. Both the answers tend to become dramatic in the end.

When did you think in the first place? Letting the mind roam is not thinking. Allowing the mind to go over and over on the same topics is not thinking.

This labelling business has gone too far like everything else.

The paper Diploma counts more than the person.

The income value determines success.

The car shows the persona. The personality is made at the gym. The clothes determine our greatness.
Where is the true thing and that's all I need.

So difficult to accept that we who wish to be remembered for the great things we did are just footprints in the sand that will wash away into oblivion as fast as we can make them. Humanity needs to grow up.

Yes. We even begin to become proud of being sicklier than others - to show how special we are and how well we are coping with it

Progress in any sphere means change of scene. Disconcerting and traumatic for those who want status quos and comfort zones.

Most of us do not even take care of our thoughts in public and act out the thoughts before we know what we are doing - speech included.

Can we force cheerfulness in our basic nature that stems from our subconscious? Yes but only if we are able to leave behind our critical fault finding and prejudiced attitudes. This is good in theory but the effort to look into one-self to see where we are not on the right positive track is something we vehemently avoid. Forced cheerfulness is like glazing over a rusted plate. No real worth in it.
The medical fact stated below is definitely true and we should all try to understand to let go, stop running the world and managing the life of other's in the guise of helping them and knowing better.

Discussions on Disturbing Issues.

Topic Number	Subject
1	No Kidding
2	The Pleasure is mine
3	Raising children on music
4	Freedom of expression
5	Contradicting lovingly
6	The older little ones
7	Conflict and competition
8	Homework from school
9	In the realm of words
10	Listen & be damned
11	Time management
12	Suicides and shooting sprees
13	The illusion of virtue
14	The illusion of honesty
15	The club of givers
16	Eyes wide shut
17	Cocksure & prejudiced
18	Saying thine part
19	Deliberately rude
20	Teaching Methodology
21	Fear of rejection
22	No time for humoring
23	Some discussions on sayings & quotes

No Kidding

I posted this agenda on face book to see what responses I would get.

I would like to start a movement with these three point agenda:

1) "NO" to having kids until you have a strong enough financial base to provide well.

2) Before marriage couples to go through a compulsory training about kids and their needs and psychology.

3) No divorce under any circumstances if there are kids.

This got me many replies and much advice. So I am sharing most of the conversations with you.

I start with this statement:

Getting my little one ready for school requires a lot of drama acting and acts that would be considered downright spoiling. She is only four-&-a-half. Being on time and such trivia has no importance for her. And we treat it as a game. Her mother has taken "spoiling" to the next level. I love the fun and mischief that goes into going to school everyday. Every morning a lot of planning goes into making the waking-up act into a theatrical performance.

Which makes me think: When we act, are we moving about with conscious thinking or simply embedded reflexes with no real thinking behind them? Are we really bringing up our child or just letting him/her grow up?

Then there is always this question on how much freedom is to be allowed, for finally the adults have to clean after them. I have realized this truth: Adults are afraid. One would think that their little world is endangered overtime a child goes experimenting or on a personal voyage of discovery. But then they are afraid of other adults too. What are they so afraid of? From what is obvious to me it is the sense of control or not having any that is so upsetting.

I have been advocating seriously that people should not have children if they do not have time or facility to bring them up and provide for them properly. I had this exchange with another face book friend and I share it - just for info:

From a reader: - If we follow your agenda then, poor people can't get married and have children.

My reply: It is the responsibility of each individual to first promote himself, become aware and make a home where the child has to come. It would be criminal to have children to perpetuate your own miserable condition onto the child.

 - I think if Allah is giving Parents the gift of a Child. This Child has a right to be born.

Allah will arrange their lives!

My reply:

Sorry do not agree. Children are the responsibility of parents. It is the result of sex that parents have for their pleasure. They have to be given a future. We should not bring in Allah. He has no role to play at this stage

My friend: Then you don't believe in this! But I do!

My reply:

I care for children. I believe in the hand of Divine intervention but I am responsible for my acts. God/Allah cannot be made responsible for everything and should not be. This becomes an easy way out to suit our convenience

Then many people came up with the objection to my contention that divorce should not be allowed. They talk of bad marriages which are in turn bad for the children. My conviction is that as long as there is this thought at the back of the mind that "we" can part, people do not make a wholehearted, concerted effort to stay together as couples; so if they have any doubts, even a shadow of one, they should not have children.

The children have a right to NOT BE born to bad parents. They have a right to life and home. The parents lose all their rights except to care & nurture the children. And finally I ask this question: Do children have rights?

On divorces, this is my view: my understanding is that at the Mother Nature level, from the occult point of view, marriage is the only state which is akin to TAPASYA that a common man experiences. It is necessary for the pair's personal growth/evolution and children born of it.

Some people contend that souls choose their place of birth and parents etc so birth should be allowed as a natural right. Now I feel this is taking expediency too far. If this premise is accepted, which I do, then the divorce will only upset the destiny of all involved; more the reason to keep the family together. Have children certainly but then keep promises made.

We say we are thinking beings. Are we? *I am completely of the opinion that we act more by custom – we may think & speak on many levels but*

51

act by tradition and inculcated habits (adapted from the writings of Francis Bacon)

Are you moving about with conscious thinking or simply embedded reflexes with no real thinking behind them? Are we really thinking beings? I feel our lives are more a display of sub-conscious control as a natural reflex in play. We need to become thinking executives to improve; consciously living and striving to live... by our most affectionate feelings & the most positive thoughts. Otherwise our marriages, our progeny and our future in today's fast-moving and complex world, we are doomed to misery.

Many of the replies I have received show the difference between what is in my mind as a resident of India in comparison to the thinking process prevalent in the western societies. When I spoke of divorce, I meant a couple and children though marriage. But many immediately picked up the cause of single parents. I must say this was never in my mind.

The question of single or double parent did not cross my mind at all.

The point in focus is the sense of responsibility and commitment with which we decide to have children and later provide them with our affection, our time and material things so that they can experience and learn about life and academics to be in control of their lives as well adjusted adults.

I see many well meaning couples, who love their children but are still making a mess of their children's lives because they have either no money or time or just no knowledge about how best to care for them.

Then I know of too many stories where the woman was left stranded with a baby by an insincere partner. This is where I want people to become more aware. If a romp in bed is all you are looking for, then so be it. Contraception is a modern day reality. Why not make sure that you are using it. You take care of yourself against the cold by wearing clothes, against dirty water by filtering it and so many other acts of care and protection. But what happens when it is a matter of a "life". Where does the sense of responsibility disappear?

Many have argued that the future is unknown so we should not lay down rules. I agree with this totally. But we should start well to begin with. Lets us plan and calculate before we bring another little one to taste the vagaries of life. There is no harm in thinking and organizing how we are going to go ahead in life; both for our sake and that of the children who are dependent on us now and on whom we shall be depending upon later.

It is also my feeling where there is affection and mutual caring; families do well even in hard times. So that is not an issue.

Point made by Rasanidhi Trivedi

I endorse your views and I am totally against divorce but unfortunately in Ahmadabad hardly 20 petitions were filed in the year 1978; now there are about 100+petitions registering daily for divorce and other matrimonial causes.

This note is important:

DIVADEEP commented on the post "No Kidding".

Yes, I fully agree to it. A couple has no right to have kids if they are not prepared financially as well emotionally. A child has to be welcomed, wanted and waited for. A child should not happen to a couple, preferably.

If man can make things happen for him and plan very well for that, whether it is marriage or festivities, he can very well prepare becoming a parent. And a good one at that. If a couple is yet to stabilize financially, they have no right to experiment with another life, and raise him/her cribbing.
For those particular about 'Allah ki deyn(gift)' well when their activities are not "Allah ki deyn", then its by-products also cannot be forced upon Allah either.

Yes, souls choose their parents. Then why not make them choose when they are wanted most. A soul would never push its birth to indifferent parents. And if so much is destiny then what will happen to our Karma account.

Before we answer our children, we have to answer to our own self 'Have I made a home for my little one? Do I have time, energy n savings for my child's long journey?' Whatever level or status of man be, the question should touch the chord at emotional level. Otherwise a mammal with 4 legs also procreates and the one with 2 legs shall also continue to contribute to an army of insecure childhood....

And I also agree that a Divorce should not happen to a family with kids.

In the worst case they may live separately but a legal divorce teaches a child too early to break a family than fix it. A choice of walking out of a difficult situation rather than healing it always keeps the foundation weak. Children need both mother and father (good or bad) otherwise they wouldn't be born of both. With a difficult parent a different set of living conditions may apply but a divorce removes any chances of recovery and puts a permanent divide in a child's psyche. And all those maintenance n security issues could be had within the marriage itself, legally   (if   condition   is   so   bad). As the saying goes 'marriages and divorces happen in the hearts' much before they happen for the outside world to see.

Kokayi Ufanifu has brought up this age-old beautiful concept that was and can still be seen in the tribal cultures all over the world. In my opinion his is the core behind a happy society.

It takes a village to raise a child. Although a child is born into a family. The child is the responsibility of the community. We must nurture them as our own, work together to create work and to do what we can to make every child who is born wanted because we celebrate life and welcome it!

LOVE is cooperation, sharing, and caring for one another!

Katherine Siswick-Clark

I do not say it is not a good idea for parents to be financially secure or to make every effort to make their marriage work, but I am also aware of the human condition. I think it comes down to what we believe. I see that a child chooses their parents, not because they want a perfect life but because they want to fully experience themselves and the entirety of their emotions, it is only through experience that which we are not that we can be experience what we are.

We come here out of choice and I believe that we make choices about what we wish for ourselves whilst we are here. At inspire a child we talk about the child's right to express themselves and be who they are, so shine their light, but if we are to say no to divorce are we then saying that when they reach adult hood or for that matter parenthood that all feelings and desires be denied? That all expression is unacceptable?

Also you say children need a mother and father good or bad, can it honestly be said that a marriage where the child is a witness or a victim of abuse of any kind is still a marriage none the less and should be continued?

I hope to teach my children to express themselves but to stay mindful and respectful of the feelings and views of others. I want them to be free to be their true selves because I believe we are all unique and wonderful parts and expressions of our creator. A child can only learn that by example and if a parent is not free to be themselves whilst of course being mindful, respectful, and compassionate and accepting of others then what are we showing our children.

We may never all agree on this subject and that is fine, we are all one, but unique all the same.

Pradeep Pk Maheshwari

Your points are well taken but I would like to regress a bit. My entire approach is on the Q - Why a child at all? Why wilfully bring a child into this world when we are not ready for it? How does it help to perpetuate our own lacunas and misery?

Of course once the child has arrived - wilfully or otherwise, then all that can be done for the child needs to be done. If divorce has to be then well it has to be.

But let us make, as a thoughtful breed, the child the centre of our lives. If we do this, our own selfishness will evaporate and divorce my never even be thought of.

Jennifer Bassett

May I add that good parents have the right to have the respect of their children? It is sad that that dispute all efforts a child grows up and then never even acknowledges father's day.

Edward Stanulevich IV

Unless the divorce is part of the destiny of the child and all involved. I think divorce should be a last choice. I would rather the child be in a broken home than a hateful home.

Pradeep Pk Maheshwari

Jennifer, My personal feeling on the Q of rights is that the parents belong to the child and not vice versa. A parent asking for respect as a right has obviously not done something right. The child was brought into this world by the parents and started with a clean slate. If later on he develops unlikeable attitudes, it is sad, but besides the God-given nature, he has definitely picked up the wrong vibes from his surroundings and parents mostly.

Edward, I agree with you. If only we had he eyes to see into somebody's destiny. Nevertheless making things easy for our egocentricity as the modern day world has done can only be condoned.

I remember a mother of a friend of mine in France, 25 years ago, complaining that her son, now a professor and nearly 40, unmarried would come home in the holidays and just sleep. She was very upset to the perceived lack of respect and consideration for her and his laziness. I explained the situation to her (as given below) to which she replied; well I never saw it this way. So I suppose it is all a matter of perspective. This is how I explained it:

No matter what the age, he comes "home" to his "mother". This is where he is "himself". It is better than going around wasting his life in bars etc etc. This is his castle where he comes for refuge. Age has nothing to do with anything here. You have obviously raised him well. He is definitely a contented person if he can sleep so easily.

Topic no 2

I give here a small write-up of mine:

The Pleasure is mine.

I have finally understood the need to spoil children. Although it is a relative term I am quite happy in letting my kid have her way. You can see in her eyes that she knows that this is HER place and that SHE is master here. The confidence that she shows when I am around vanishes with others, including her own mother who is a little more stoic in her responses and not averse to impose rules and conditions that to the baby may seem draconian.

The other day one of my friends from France was here with me and spent some days with us. We were talking about the responsibilities of raising children and how to best fulfil them. In passing he mentioned that he had noticed that I rarely censor, forbid or discipline my child; rather I tend to go along with the child. He wondered if this would not o eventually lead to spoiling the girl. Well, I told him it is my belief that we all need a friend who would accept us as we are without judging us and I was being that to my child. To the child the parents should be the friends in front of who he can be himself/herself. If I want to stop her from doing something, I do so by diverting her attention.

This attitude needs to be nurtured. If we become too much of the teacher or the disciplinarian we risk alienating the relationship and a heavy price would have to be paid later in life if a great distance and distrust gets created between the parent and child. So I told him that even though I was behaving in the manner as he had remarked there was nothing, at least not I, stopping him to take the action he thought best. If he felt a little show of displeasure or correction was warranted, I would be glad that he showed it. The child should learn that everybody was not the same and it would be honestly a big mistake to protect the child too much from the big bad world. I want that everyone took the liberty to behave with my child as they thought best. Let the child see the world in all its facets from the word go. This was in its best interest.

If, of course, things went too much out of hand then I would be there for her and step in as a barrier. I am and shall always be the island where the child is protected and told the secrets of life. My job is to explain the tragedies and teach her the tricks of life. The ideal is that I change my style with her growing. As she grows and her stances change, so should my behaviour and responses. Parents who are able to do this will never have much to complain.

With me it is "no holes barred" exploration of the world. Her every spore wants to explore and play. There is no fear and her strong will is unwavering. She is demanding and expects obedience unquestioned. What is wrong in this in this harsh world? We ask this of our grown children but stop them in their tracks, kill all incentive and stifle them before they get a chance to flower. The truth is that we stop the child when it is not convenient to us. The child is not here for our convenience. Period.

Note: there is no deliberate mischief in her. Just play and of course wanting to play at all the games she sees us playing. Her ability to ape is astounding. She is a keen observer and repeats every action she sees us do in one shot.

Everyone wants to know why I am spoiling her. My question is am I? She needs to play and explore this world - right? And I am letting her do it. How else will she know what is OK and what is not?!!!!!

But I must say, having her in my arms or when she comes and envelops me in her arms or recompenses me with a kiss, the experience transposes me out of myself and my heart melts into chocolate syrup and blows up out of proportion like a Goodyear airship.

It is such a lovely feeling to be the chosen one. I have never been loved liked this. The smile and her tinkling laughter are worth it all. Not only hers, for that matter any child's. Let us not become so staid that we lose all sense of the fun of life.

PS: But I have not lost my head yet. I am now teaching her to take me a little more seriously and show my displeasure through my eyes + shake of my head. I must say that she is beginning to recognize and respect this.

It has to be made as a request or tears will flow, backed highly dramatized acting- and make me feel like a jerk. I know I am being manipulated but then my mother, wife, colleagues and everyone I know is doing it so what is new? I just wait for my opportunity to have my own tantrums one of these days.

Richard Schooping:

Lovely; and yes, when we harness love with love, love then leads in love. Children are love's response to creation and so just as seeds, it is how we nurture that determines the yielded fruit.

Megha Pushpendra: what a feeling....

..I have to learn this...the child is not here for our convenience....

very good write up Mr.Maheshwari..looking forward to more..

Katherine Siswick-Clark responds with and I agree:

I see where you are coming from and certainly having a child is not something to be taken lightly, I am all for preparing and doing all we can for our children. I am just aware that people don't realise the enormity of having a child often until they have had them and our biology goes a long way in creating the desire to have children. There are so many reasons why people bring children into the world.

I feel that each circumstance is different for each couple and family. I think children are ultimately the centre of most family's lives, but life does sometimes interfere with that and complicate the simple truths. Parents have their own issues too, their own baggage so to speak some of that only comes to the surface as a result of having a family of their own and the pressures and lessons that that bring. Its the responsibility of the parent to deal with their stuff and to be there for their child, but in my view I think parents, communities, governments, nations need to pull together to help parents. We need to be supportive, accepting and compassionate, for only when parents love and feel good about themselves will this make the difference. It is not about imposing rules or making examples of people or their behaviors and bringing about feelings of resentment, guilt and shame, in my mind it's about uniting and guiding through love, patience, compassion and acceptance...exactly the things we say is important for children.

.

This note by Paul Schmolke is what I totally agree to:

Mindfulness of what we do is the answer to this dilemma. Mindfulness should include being aware of the present and future consequences of our actions. Yes the future is unknown except within our own ego's but if we look inside and see the trouble caused by our own actions as if they were directed at us then the answers become clear. Being mindful translate as understanding the motivations for our actions and weighing them against our own realities. Do this on a moment by moment basis.

MINDFULLness. (Pradeep's note)

Our 5 senses are recording many inputs all the time. How much of it registers? The human mind trains itself to filter inputs in such a way that we see and hear only that which goes along with our wishes and desires.

Therefore in the final analysis it is our desire/wish centre that controls our lives. Not our thinking and reasoning centre.

For the present moment in Earth's history the mind and Reason are acting as slaves to the Desire Centre.

This has to change. We shall be master of ourselves only when we consciously become master of acts and do not allow any other influence to sway us.

Right now everything influences us through the subconscious. The weather, the sound, the words, the scenes --- everything .

We are virtually living outside of ourselves and buffeted by external stimuli all the time and we permit it to register in us and decide things for us.

This has to stop if we are to be ourselves. Right now we are a part of the collective.

We can call ourselves individuals only when we can say with guarantee that our acts have origin only in our innermost being.

This reply needs a serious read:

Globbler: Wonderful topic, Pradeep!

I recently read an eye-opening abstract regarding reason from Swami Vivekananda:

"When there is a conflict between the heart and the brain, let the heart be followed, because intellect has only one state, reason, and only within reason does intellect work, it cannot go beyond it. It is the heart that takes one to the highest plane, which the intellect can never reach; it goes beyond intellect and reaches to what is called inspiration. Intellect can never become inspired; only the heart, when it is enlightened, becomes inspired. It is always the heart that speaks in the man or woman of love; it discovers a greater instrument that the intellect can give you, the instrument of inspiration. Just as the intellect is the instrument of knowledge, so is the heart the instrument of inspiration. However, in a lower state, the heart is a much weaker instrument than the intellect. An ignorant person knows nothing, for he lives in the lower emotions. Properly cultivated, the heart will be elevated, and will go beyond intellect; there, it will be changed into inspiration. Everyone will go beyond intellect in the end.

If you are pure, you will reach God. "Blessed are the pure in heart, for they shall see God." It is the pure heart that reaches the goal. A pure heart sees beyond the intellect; it knows things that reason can never know. ("The heart has its reasons which reason knows nothing of." – Blaise Pascal). Whenever there is conflict between the pure heart and the intellect, always side with the pure heart, even if you think that your heart is unreasonable.

The pure heart is the best mirror for the reflection of truth. As soon as it is pure, all truths flash upon it in an instant; all truth in the universe will manifest in your heart, if you are sufficiently pure…. It is the cultivation of the heart, and not the intellect, that will lessen the misery of the world.

Intellect has been cultivated, with the result that hundreds of sciences have been discovered, and their effect has been that the few have made slaves of the many. Artificial wants have been created; and every person, whether he has money or not, desires to have those wants satisfied, and when he cannot, he struggles and dies in the struggle. Through the intellect is not the way to solve the problem of misery, but through the heart. If all this vast amount of effort had been spent in making people purer, gentler, and more forbearing, this world would have a thousand-fold more happiness than it has today. So always cultivate the heart, for only through the heart does the Lord speak."

A few words from Richard Schooping.

Yes, much is happening, and much is also not happening. Weather, energies, cultures, etc.. These are the changing qualities of nature that always occur, no matter the form nature takes. So we are not here to perfect anything. We are to realize that all is perfect now. These continual attempts to "fix" things is simply our mind dancing within our awareness, yet we are more.

It is through a continual surrender of our beliefs (what we think about these things) that we realize more than the mind. Again, the mind wants to create some new and amazing structure so it once and for all can finally fix everything, but this is illusion. The more we neutrally observe the more harmonics that are revealed; nothing is happening but our reaction to our experience, and so let us address our reaction.

And so concerning marriage and children what I shared also applies. The more we each are present the more presence that now is aware of the love that it is through the many as a real-world example: when we are in a battle, be it amongst soldiers on foreign land, with another person, with our lover, with our children, etc... This is the ego. The ego is battling over some ownership, but what it does not realize is that all of this is only a projection from within itself, and so it is only fighting over illusions. And when two egos are now at war they are always at war as war only creates more war. We never win a war, we only destroy each other enough to realize the ultimately futility of the ego's actions. And when we are at war we are either offensive or defensive in our reaction to the war and so how will this resolve? How do we transcend the war when within a war mentality?

The question is not how to win the war or fix the battle, as this is just more battle. The question is, "what is the way beyond this battle?" the way to realize more is through presence. Presence is that which observes any ego reaction. When we are present we are analogous to a person watching a battle from a ledge above. They have a clearer vantage point. They recognize greater patterns at play and so they do not react as the ego, they respond as a greater love. (from *PK: what I would have called – become a witness to ourselves*)

This is what I am now sharing, that all of this reaction to our experience only creates more reaction to our experience and herein is the loop we become stuck in; but, when we let ALL of our battles go and we pause and observe we realize more than the ego and more than any battle, including within our relationships with our lovers, our children, and our world.

This note is worth noting:

Katherine Siswick-Clark:

I see what you are saying Pradeep, and I think that sometimes marriage is easy to enter and exit, however no one can know what will happen in the future and I think that most people that do commit to marriage intend it to last, but as I said circumstances and people change and children should certainly be considered in all areas of family life and what is best for them should be a deciding factor. The fact is I think that in some instances divorce is best for the children and that a loveless marriage full of anger, bitterness and resentment is not where children should be. In an ideal world there would be no divorce, but that is not the nature of this planet in my opinion, we are spiritual beings living here to experience every aspect of ourselves and decide who we are. Whilst we are here on this planet we have a human condition to contend with. I think our children choose their parents before they arrive here for their own personal growth. Children have the right to be heard and consulted and we have a duty to protect them and guide them the best we can. It is my belief that children are highly perceptive and they pick up their parent's emotions and a marriage that is not working and cannot be salvaged is evident to a child and I think that children are happy when their parents are too. I just hope that when couples do part they respect one another and protect their children, that they don't use the children against the other parent.

One of my dear friends wrote this lovely mail and I give it here verbatim:

<u>Paul Schmolke</u>

As someone who has been married for 43 years, and is childless by choice, I made two of these commitments early on. My wife and life partner Lynne spent a big chunk of her adult life working with abused, neglected and psychologically damaged children trying to help them through some terrible times. My father, also a psychologist, was involved with children who had been committed to state mental institutions because they were damaged beyond repair. None of the children that either of them treated, managed or helped had any choice in how they came out or who their parents were. In most cases, the parents were in the same situation and did the normal thing and repeated their parent's mistakes with flawed marriages and distorted points of view. None of them were intrinsically bad and none of them understood what they were doing or why, they were merely repeating what they had either seen or been told. Short of sterilization, none of this could have been avoided as the emotionally or psychologically damaged people of the planet still have the biological mandate to reproduce. This is part of being an animal.

We try to help by being "adoptive" parents for kids that aren't doing too well with their families or have lost their families or have been discarded by their families.

Reproductive choices are largely dictated by our animal nature and as such are substantially beyond the reach of reason. Churches have tried to intervene or influence, legislative bodies have done the same. Society in general has worked long and hard to try and demonize premarital physical relations, unwed motherhood, "illegitimate children", etc. You cannot legislate this area of human behavior because it is beyond the control of the very people that are seen as the problem and that could fix it.

Each of us individually has the responsibility to take charge of our own existence and do the best we can based on what we have been taught or what we have learned from our peers. Some of our activities will not be pleasing to others and some will make mistakes with themselves, their spouses and their children. This is human nature.

Do children deserve better? Certainly they do. We can't know the ultimate outcome of anyone's reproductive or parenting experience until we see the end product - the adult. We can try to influence the young but we are doing battle with the reproductive urge and it is more powerful than anything else that I know of.

The ideas you express are wonderful and I will predict your success raising your child as it is clear that love, respect, admiration and awe are present in you. Trying to influence others here is unimaginably difficult as the urge to make more people will not be denied and at about 14 in the USA, we start to see the problem. In my home town, where it is commonplace for young women to have children out of wedlock, the girls' family usually takes over some of the responsibilities as they know that to do otherwise would be very bad for the child. We have quite a few extended families here. It seems a shame but most of the young ones come out OK in time and many of the mothers manage to finish school and improve their lives. Could they do better? Absolutely! Can they control their reproductive urge? Absolutely not! Can we help? Absolutely! Teach them everything you can and help them to see good paths to travel.

As far as divorce is concerned, I enjoy keeping promises and I love long term relationships. It takes the courage of your convictions and the will to keep a promise and while not always fun, it is always rewarding. More than a few of my friends have been with me for 60 years. My wife and I have been together as friends for 45 years and married for 43 of them.

On the question of children's rights etc

Melanie Moore Ph D:

Children most certainly do have "rights", single parents are not bad parents however...

At this time when the evolution of consciousness is taking place and the old paradigms of thought breaking down I do feel we must challenge our boundaries in thinking further.

The beliefs which say the only way to parent correctly is with two parents of the opposite sex is constriction rather than expansion....

The reason I mention this is because it alienates people whom do not conform to 1 MAN 1 WOMAN and 2.2 CHILDREN... besides I believe the human race is spiritually evolving towards androgyny and that marriage is a mainly religious ideal that is not now relevant. As long as love is at the core it doesn't matter and children can be well nurtured...

Children choose who they are going to be born through at a soul level, so they make their choices there.

Pradeep Pk Maheshwari

For one I never said anything about single parents. Secondly it is not a question of single or double parents at all. It is our sense of responsibility which is the focus.

From all the replies and notes I am receiving one thing is becoming clear. You are all talking only at the level of mentally advanced and educated/aware people.

Whereas I am talking at the general level of humanity at large - which is quite at the educated chimpanzee level or so to say.

I agree with you on the choices the souls make.

Here is another mail from my friend Susan Connors that is worth a serious read.

Hi PK!

This is such wonderful contemplation that I stopped working to read the whole email.

74

I wholeheartedly agree with you on points 1 and 2. On the third point, I think it makes a great deal of difference whether one of the parents is equipped to raise a child or children on their own. I have seen many successful single parent homes and many unsuccessful 2-parent homes.

To your first point -- in general, poor people receive less than adequate education and thus access to birth control information and sex education. But, there is in almost everyone an emotional need to be successful at something. For many poor young women they think this means motherhood which often ends in child abandonment whether to a relative or 'the system' which does a very poor job of raising children.

So, financial success and reproductive responsibility are both related to education. We can either remove the radical 'religionists' (who fear children being taught about sex instead of fearing their children's' ignorance) from making it difficult, if not impossible, for sex education to be provided in school or we can start tying tubes in young women as soon as they start to menstruate and/or "vasectomies" boys when they enter puberty. The latter would allow teens to have recreational sex without fear of procreation, but what society would ever pass laws that are so intrusive to an individual's rights? We may actually have to consider this at some point for the sake of the world due to overpopulation or we can get busy providing quality education for everyone. Those who don't want to go to school can have their tubes tied, etc. or be confined to a same-sex community-service facility that also provides sex education. Radical?

Not really. Not when the children that are born cannot be taken care of; not when 25,000 people a day die of starvation in this overpopulated world.

I do disagree with your friend who says that sex is for pleasure. Sex is for procreation first which is nature's intent. The fact that in humans it is also pleasurable (and the fact that we have no natural enemies but ourselves and diseases that 'Mom Nature' cooks up) is why, as intelligent as we are, we suffer from overpopulation, whereas other species most often do not.

To your second point -- Absolutely. Child rearing education should be mandatory for any couple that can potentially bare children. Marital education should be compulsory as well as should a "cooling off" period where young couples must stay apart long enough for the hormones to calm down and the individuals can decide whether they really want to marry the other person for all of the right reasons.

This may all make it sound as though I don't believe in God/Allah, but I do. I believe that we were "given" free will so that we could learn, individually and collectively, from our mistakes and grow intellectually and spiritually. That is also why parenting is so important because until a child has the ability to reason, the child's 'free will' must be restrained and contained and good behavior nurtured for the safety of the child.

Thanks for the opportunity to think and respond, PK. We often don't know how we really feel about something until we are forced to focus on the subject. This was a good break from work.............Susan.

A general reply by Katherine Siswick-Clark:

Thank you Pradeep for your thoughts. I can see where you are coming from and I see your good intentions with what you are proposing... what you say about being financial secure is important, although I think often parents don't fully realise the cost involved in raising a child, but nevertheless some fore thought is good in and ideal world.

In regards to your second thought I feel that it is good for couples to have some experience of what it is to be a parent before they become one, although in my experience nothing prepares you for the changes it brings. I did a lot of research and I planned carefully before with good nutrition, health checks and when I did get pregnant I read lots of information, got our home in order, work etc...did lots of mediation prepared myself well I thought, but then my son arrived and it was like a tornado had come through my life and everything was left upside down. Each experience is so unique there is only so much preparation you can do in my experience.

Your third point about no divorce, I do disagree with because I think that the ideal is a solid family where the parents are united in love and respect, but people change and children change a relationship too and if couples grow apart and there is no way that the marriage and relationship can be salvaged then I feel it is better for the children that they go their separate ways. There are so many children hurt as a result of parents staying together out of obligation and feeling resentment and this is not healthy for the children. I do feel that if parents choose to part they should do everything in their power to do so amicably and show their children they have respect for the child's mother/father and they should certainly make every effort to be there for their child and ensure they know that they are loved no matter what. If done correctly children can survive marriage breakups without long term scars, in fact it can prove a beneficial learning experiences. Out of all the hardships we encounter there is something good to be found.

Those are just my opinions, I would love to hear others thoughts.

On a general matter of opinion, I had this remark to put forth:

To say the truth I don't see disagreements anywhere. Life is not a question of agreements/arguments and such. It is realising that we have not seen the whole as yet. So we share information and hopefully, learn from it.

After reading many of the comments received on divorce:

Finally I see that the level of humanity we are, it is best to separate. The harm done by separation is less than by living in a terrorised atmosphere but it would be nice if we could rise to the occasion and grow stronger to win over our failings.

I suppose the experiences that will come forth are part of the destinies of both parents and children.

Megha Pushpendra commented :

""NO" to having kids until you have a strong enough financial base to provide well.

enunciate "enough" Mr.maheshwari.

Providence is subjective as well..it's God's activity..let's not mess up with him...I disagree with the statement. We don't have kids we are blessed with them. The matter ends there and starts from there... Let's think laterally on this issue..it ramifies..just a strong desire to give them the best in the world that is in our area of influence is "enough" for me.....

My will (not my wish)to see a twinkle in my "doing in life" would bring in the providence......

The school of life is anytime better than "Eton"....and doesn't charge anything..or does it?...

My comment- I have yet to see anything coming free. Life makes you pay dearly for every lesson.

"Before marriage couples to go through a compulsory training about kids and their needs and psychology."

....I agree...tell me if you develop this....I can help..

" No divorce under any circumstances if there are kids"…………..

Hearts get married....rest all are details..."

"respected sir.. i deliberately did not read any of the comments before writing...........we all are functions of circumstances....perspectives in this serious an issue could have served as interfering radical.."

Comment by Pradeep maheshwari:

 I am led to conclude that humanity is not ready to think otherwise. It is perfectly happy with things as they are. Of course most would want adjustments to make things more conducive to their heart's desire but too much change or too radical an approach seems scary. I suppose I will let myself be swayed for now.

A comment by Richard Schooping:

Children are clay and are shaped by the environment they "enter" into, and also there are no accidents as each birth is within a resonant tapestry of love and so less what ifs and more what now, let each one deepen into themselves, and then more than mind is discovered. Concerning divorce, again, the mind thinks it has all of the answers and can tell all what to do, but this is a mind-made fallacy. We are not to be led by the mind in our relations as this is like asking the moon for sunlight, it won't happen. We are to now let harmony be our guide because this is what we truly are – "one harmonic awareness" dancing as forms. If we listened to the mind we would be divorced, and then married, and then divorced, and then married, ad infinitum, and so we realize the futility with this. Let harmony guide and continue to listen to the heart. It is when we listen to and act as the ego that we then experience drama after drama. But, when we observe our entire experience with less mind (including in marriages with children) our experience blooms and reveals more than the mind grasps to understand.

My comment on the above passage

From the vantage point of absolute truth, I agree with you and my understanding of the situation is the same. But look at the level of the gross animal which is where the change is required.

We are doing everything to indulge in our passions and our reasonings and actions are all aimed at fulfilling our desires.

The Earth today is poisoned and mutilated because of it.

So I feel a little control and a little education needs to be pressed on the uncontrolled living that we see.

The passage that you have written above will only give more ammunition to those who would rather enjoy the moment instead of quietening down, reflect and impose any-self discipline.

Paul Schmolke commented

"Maybe we are our own best teachers after all. We are shown all the right answers from a very young age. All we need to do then is learn how to apply them. I think most people know the right answers but just don't understand that the answers apply to them. "

I add this note to the above:

On this subject I had a very eye-opening experience. My wife was visiting a mystic for she was keen to have a child. When we came in front of him the crowd had left so we had a quiet moment. The crowd I had seen was just using him for their minor desires and even ailment to be taken care of. The conversation veered towards helping people who were not ready to lift a finger for their own emancipation.

His reply was: I know that they are fooling with me. I can see that you too have the sight. What would you do? They are children and I feel like helping them out.

- I told him that it was my feeling that this expending of energy for useless results would only make him sick and tired eventually and if these people are to be helped he should use his position to make them act & do rather than what he was presently doing which was a colossal waste of good energy

His reply was: I know that they are using me. At the bottom of their being they know what the problem is but they are not prepared to take cognizance of it or lift a finger. So if I can I help them out.

- My response was: You are only spoiling them and making them weaker. Help them to rise above their limitations. Teaching them will do much more in the long run. There is nothing like a little suffering to goad one on.

etc etc

Later I heard that he died soon after.

Ana Prpic:

Pradeep, first of all, thank you for this topic.

It breaks my heart and tears come in my eyes when my 16 years daughter slams the door and tells me she hates me, because I won't let her go out on a school day until her grades in school improve. I have to be very strong not to give in and remind myself constantly that she'll be over it in an hour or two. Her words >I hate you!< are like a knife in my heart, but she's a teenager and that's what teenagers do. I have agreements with my children, we work on them together, and in general, she's allowed to do more, stay out longer, etc., then many of her friends. She went to a rock concert in another country last year; only one more of her friends was allowed to do that. But she knows that, while she has bad grades in school and failing subjects, she can't go out on a school day, only on weekends, no matter what. That's the agreement, and I'll give her any help she needs with studying, but I can't study for her. If she's lazy to study, on continuing basis, she knows there are consequences.

She's very difficult in that respect, much more than her brother, when it comes to making it her way she's capable of crying, begging, kissing, and all sorts of things she thinks might break me. But I feel that setting boundaries and consistency are very important. Listening, talking, explaining, spending time with your child, especially as Edward said, spending it with awareness, these are, in my opinion, as much important.

As I said, I'd rather be a friend to her and let her go out as often as she wants to, it would be easier for me, but in the long run it's not good for her. I'd rather she slams the doors now than curse me later. A daughter of a friend of mine, whose father died and the mother lets her do anything she wants, told me once she'd rather have curfew `coz then she'll know her mother cares for her. If you start behaving like a friend to your child they might think that it's all the same to you what's going on with them and that sense of insecurity could be very dangerous.

So, these are my experiences, and I'd love to hear more. Never too late to learn something new when it comes to kids. Well, anything actually.:)

Few words by Edward Stanulevich IV

One of the biggest problems here in the USA is that children no longer have respect for their elders. The ability to control and discipline (root word disciple, as in to teach) has been undermined by child abuse advocates. Abuse under any name is wrong, but children do need boundaries.

As a child, I was given the opportunity to learn and grow on my own. I had limits I was given, but for the most part my mother let me learn my lessons myself. As I got older and more responsible, I was given more freedom. Strict discipline was rarely needed with me.

Every child is different. Some you can do this with. Others, like my step-son, you cannot. He is 12, and by his age I was more or less taking care of myself. I did not have to cook my own food all the time, or do my own laundry, but most of what I needed done, I did. I was also left alone at home without any problems.

He is very different from me when I was his age. He is still trying to explore his world, but does so with little thought of self-preservation. He was recently punished for banging a can of body spray on a nail. Why did he do it? No one knows! He is lucky he did not get hurt. He does stuff like this a lot when not supervised.

We are working on developing some sense of independence in him. We are also trying to get him to see that he will be able to have much more fun if we can trust him. Which for the most part, he has proven we cannot. We got three different stories about what happened to the can of body spray before we got him to tell the truth.

I have demonstrated to him on a few occasions, that if he starts telling lies, we will not be able to believe him when he is telling the truth. This is a big part of being able to trust him.

We are also working on his disrespecting his mother. He was allowed to run all over her when his father left. She did not have the energy to control him. Her ex-husband was disrespectful to her, and so the boy has followed suit. We are working on showing him that you can still have fun and joke around, while being respectful to his mother.

I have seen parents go down the road of letting their kids run the show. My wife was doing that with him for a while. We have only six short years left to teach him to take care of himself. Being your child's parent is more important than being their friend. She has tried to be his friend, and he just ran all over her. He has not learned in the process. Now, she is being his parent, and he is doing much better in life because of it.

Fun is an important part of bonding with your child. So is discipline & mutual respect. Open communication. Your parents are the first and most important people to show you how to treat others, and how you should expect others to treat you.

PK's note

Being friends does not mean not laying down rules and demarcating boundaries. We have to teach them how society lives by some norms. But as you would see in my original write-up, I am laying the foundation early. I see a lot of parents shouting, criticising, threatening and putting down their foot but not conversing - this is disaster in the making.

Even at the age of 4+, I explain my point of view to the little one does not feel left out and my firm no is made to be respected. But then I offset this by doing something unexpected like buying her an ice-cream when she least expected it and she knows that she is loved and cared for although I am tough with her sometimes.

It all boils down to how much respect we have given to the child right from the beginning.

Edward Stanulevich IV

The path of explaining your rules to your child can be a hard and time consuming one. If you can do it, it works great. As they get older, they will test their boundaries. That is human nature. They will always want to know why you have placed this boundary here and that boundary there.

Parents often forget that they are first and foremost a teacher to their children!

Ana, your daughter sounds like a healthy, normal teenager!!! You must be doing a good job if she says she "hates" you.

I think that is how teens say "thank you."

Topic No 3

Raising Children on Music,

While on the subject of raising children, an important factor can be music. It has been noticed and even studied that children brought up surrounded by classical music are more balanced, tolerant and relaxed in the demeanour. They are not so easily disturbed and show reflective attitudes.

Whereas children exposed to cacophonous sounds and milieu grow up with violent & vulgar tendencies. Would more likely be superficial and have tendency to bully.

So I would safely say that from the parenting view-point, it is the vibes with which we surround them from their day of conception that matters: if our demeanour is harsh or soft even though we love them, it will show accordingly later in their personas. Do we treat them with respect and intelligently or as all-knowing adults who have to be obeyed – can make the whole difference in their disposition later on. In similar vein I can go on but I am sure you would have got my meaning.

In passing I would like to add this story I read long ago. An older lady was looking for a used car. A friend who went along with here noticed that the first thing she would do is to start the radio. She could not hide her curiosity and asked he reason because the old lady was seemingly not interested in the motor or such other things as we would normally be. The old lay explained that she puts on the radio to see which station the radio is normally fixed on. If it is on classical music, then the chances are that the car has been run sedately and maintained affectionately and therefore would be the better option among others.

I remember my own initiative to bring the sense of music to my daughter. I found by hits and misses that she liked Elvis Presley which is also my favourite too. I would pick her up in my arms from the time she was 8 months old and we would dance to Elvis. Her gurgles of contentment were obvious. Then gradually I introduced both Indian and western classical music too. I can say with pride, that we have never known tantrums but yes she is metamorphosing into a young lady who knows her mind and she argues her point; she takes no nonsense and neither gives us any.

Megha Pushpendra

sure sir....when i conceived my son ..from garbh sanskaar to Mozart i heard everything...used to see such lovely dreams..can never forget them.. they float in my eyes every now and then.....whatever i am today..my son has groomed me..he is bringing me up.......

regards

Katherine Siswick-Clark commented:

"Thank you Pradeep for sharing :)

I think music is a wonderful tool for helping children to express themselves and it works on all levels of their being. I love many types of music, although I am not a huge fan of classical; however that said I did play classical music to my children when I was pregnant with them and I have since then. I do listen to the music I like around the home, I think if you like a particular music our children recognise that and they enjoy how it uplifts and makes us feel I think. I also play a lot of children music and I have taken both my children to music groups which they have really enjoyed.

I think instruments and music helps a child to connect with their bodies, mind, emotions and their souls. I think it is good if children can be exposed to all forms of music as it helps to appreciate diversity and discover what appeals to them. I also think drums are wonderful for children, all sound is healing in my opinion, but drums have a really special quality and many health benefits too.

Thank you for raising this subject.

Topic No 4

Freedom of Expression

Here is another of my remarks that started another round of meaningful discussion:

On the Q of freedom of expression to children: Adults are afraid. One would think that their little world is endangered every time a child goes experimenting or on a personal voyage of discovery. But then they are afraid of other adults too. What are they so afraid of?

Katherine Siswick-Clark :

Yes I think adults are afraid because they fear how they will be received by others. Many adults are self conscious, afraid of being excluded or being on the outside, of being different, and I think these filters down to the children. I think adults today fear their children not being accepted, being bullied, and as a result experimenting is a fearful prospect for what would others say about it...really we should be teaching our children that we are all unique aspects of one. Difference is to be seen, celebrated and appreciated, that our difference is our greatness. We are all unique, just like everything in nature is unique and its ok and wonderful to be so, for it is our nature to be and we need to explore and experience as much or ourselves as we can and express our truth for that is our very purpose for being.

Katherine Siswick-Clark

I just wanted to thank you again Pradeep, you gave me inspiration for my blog. Bless you for your wonderful insights, it is a honor to have you share your wisdom with us

Pradeep Pk Maheshwari

This is overwhelming. As you would have seen I try to make people think by raising question rather than throw quotes and thoughts for the day at them. Without a bit of churning......without a live question, answers are pointless.

Paul Schmolke

Childern have been taught no cultural or social bias. They are open and honest. I can't imagine anything that will produce more fear in the heart of most adults than honesty and openness.

Katherine Siswick-Clark

This is a very good point Paul. Often I think we fear the truth because it seems easier and simpler to carry on as we are than to face up to the reality and make the change. The change itself can be the fear. Perhaps this is something else we need to help our children with so that they won't have these same fears, and they will instead embrace change as they know it is for our highest good and is about growth and is that not why we came here in the first place? As I was told by Neale Donald Walsch, evolution only goes in one direction! It would seem to me then that there is nothing to fear...only love is real...we just need to remind ourselves of this fact when confronted with fear. Thank you Paul for sharing your wonderful insight, sharing our individual perspectives really opens up our minds and our world.

Paul Schmolke

I'll never forget being a child. The images and memories are vivid and, happy or sad, they remind me of unvarnished reality. I can even remember conversations with my invisible friend Joey that took place when I was about 3 years old in 1948. I can remember the sunshiny day in 1950 when I met my lifelong friend Rick. I can remember a lot of other stuff too but the things I remember most nowadays are the discoveries of hypocrisy when I started to grow out of childhood and into whatever it is that comes next. It was at this point that I now wish my parents would have handed me a copy of Sun Tzu's Art of War so I could have recognized my innocence for what it was and looked over the long standing realities that comprise civilizations feeble attempts at consideration for non-self or the other.

I know that Pradeep understands this dilemma and you seem to as well. My greatest fear now is that I will be misunderstood. Language is such a clumsy tool for expressing what's really inside - but I do try as best I can. Thanks.

Katherine Siswick-Clark

Pradeep, you certainly have a way to get people thinking...thank you

Katherine Siswick-Clark:

Paul it is wonderful that you have such vivid memories, childhood is a precious time and certainly the realities of the world in which we live can come as a shock to us when we are small. Our eyes open to a world full of contradictions and as you put so well, hypocrisy. However I feel that we are going through a transformation, people are awakening to what is not working in our world and to who they really are. You are right in what you say Paul about our language. Words often seem insufficient for the depth of thought and feeling we wish to convey, but I feel that our intention is the best communicator and when we speak from our heart what needs to be said will be said and you can not control how that is interpreted, people will always hear and see what they wish to. Jesus was a wonderful messenger, but there are always those who use his words for their own ends and those that are still fighting about what he meant, we can only speak our truth and know that we have played our part and all is happening as it should be. Thank you giving us all something to ponder

Pradeep Pk Maheshwari

Paul's points have poignancy. I feel Control as a natural reflex is in play. We need to become thinking executives to improve; consciously living and striving to live by our most affectionate feelings & the most positive thoughts.

Paul Schmolke

I think the need for control arises out of fear - of which there are many possibilities. Sun Tzu's ideas can easily be translated or converted to peaceful and loving ways as I perceive them to be universal means of dealing with any situation that may arise. His primary rule is to avoid fighting. His ideas about analysis of what is presented to us and how to most effectively deal with it underlie a lot of western thought in spite of being well over 2,000 years old and of Asian/Chinese origin. I don't know that I consider it to be a good model for dealing with everything in my everyday life but I can see its utility in many other circumstances. Like many aspects of Western political activity it has been abused, twisted and misappropriated for the needs of some that are greedy or self serving. They will be with us forever.

Pradeep Pk Maheshwari

On this I have much to say but all I can say in short is that the message of Love, Charity and spreading the word as espoused by Christian philosophy, allowed for a lot of manipulation by clever people. We need to teach about the beauty of the garden but also the scorpion under the rock.

Paul Schmolke

I understand exactly what you are saying and I agree completely. I read a lot of history and philosophy on spiritual matters and am appalled at the lack of understanding that a great many people have regarding their culturally based spiritual connections. When I look at the age of mankind's foundation writings and read the ideas, that were expressed, sometimes thousands of years ago, by these very insightful authors I am amazed at how much has been known and for how long. I am saddened by how much of it has been perverted by modern societies. My doubts were first raised when I was four years old on a Sunday morning that I will never forget. About 15 years ago, I started to study Buddhism and then Zen. I am still studying and still sitting but my feelings and ideas have become more generalized. I have concluded that I will follow a path to gain understanding and promote harmony and good feelings when called upon. I'm not sure where the path will lead and since it represents the future, I can't really know but intuitively, I'm sure it's the right answer for me as it seeks to do good and promote friendship and good will. I think actions speak louder than words.

Treat everyone with respect no matter how humble they may be. Show compassion in your actions towards others. Try to help if you are able. Work to understand things as they are.

Teya Slo

Congratulations to you all on this totally wonderful conversation! I can just - agree.

Topic no 5

Contradicting Lovingly

Pradeep Pk Maheshwari:

97

When I was young, in college and still sorting out the everyday contradictions in terms of human relationships, one of the features of my life was to understand the attitude of my parents towards me. From one angle it was clear that I was precious to them and from another angle, they seem to take me for a nincompoop. At one end of the spectrum I was supposed to do them proud by coming up to some standards that were never clearly defined while at the same time I was not supposed to show any initiative and do what I was told. On this point the directions were clear: as if the parents were saying "We are here and know what is best for you. We are doing the thinking for you, all that is needed will be provided; you; just be a nice, sweet chubby child, the apple of our eyes." As if they had never bargained for the child to grow and assert some of his own personality.

When this time did come, it changed into a period of confrontation. It became a competition between two diametrically opposite tendencies. One set in their ways, afraid of change and the other experimenting and exploring, feeding and thriving on change. Eventually the situation came to a pass where all listening came to a stop. Every sentence of my father began with a "NO". This puzzled me to no end and unfortunately nobody was giving me the right honest answers either.

Then one day I went to somebody's house and there I saw a sticker. It showed an older cranky looking man shouting at an obviously younger child: "The answer is No. Now what did you want?" This was the beginning of wisdom finally coming into my life. I realized that a sticker made in the USA, if so universal in its character, is floating around then certainly this attitude of my parents which was puzzling me, is more universally prevalent than is honestly accepted. A little more close observation of all the parents around me, backed by reading The Reader's Digest made the answers come tumbling into my life.

Today into my late adult life, I am astonished to see how much this tendency to negate and contradict permeates life in general. As I see it, the seeds are sown when the child is growing into an adult and the parents are not grasping this fact in its entirety. They want to protect him and shield him. In their zeal they don't want him to act at all, as if this way they can protect him from all adversity. The child on the other hand begins first by seething inside and then hiding his true self and living a double life; so to say. The parents get more and more strongly into the denying and the child starts even more vehemently saying No to it. Is it any wonder that the adult who results is afraid that his life will be taken over and therefore learns to say No to everything. His relationships are all difficult; whatever kind it may be- professional, amicable or amorous. This way he gets into a perennial "denial" mode. This perverted character then gets passed on from generation to generation.

Look around closely. How often do you see people agreeing and accepting each other and in comparison how often we are crossing each other out?

I remember when I was just entering teenage; I was trying to paint a sunset. My father's comment on seeing my attempts was that I being a child should try to paint subjects more suitable to my age. But I kept on which upset him and finally got what I wanted, appreciated by others or not. In my case the story has a happy ending. Eventually, many years later, I painted a canvas which before even it was dry; my father took it and hung it in his room. This was appreciation of a high order.

Fate had a hand in my upbringing. I had the good luck to grow into an adult far away from the restrictive and limited scope of my home. I had an international exposure and had teachers who were always listening and ready to help me find the answers to MY questions; without the bias of social norms restricting our exchanges.

Yet sadly my father never got over his habit of taking the opposite side to any exchange of idea, conversation or suggestion. It was so sad. I wanted so much to converse and share my life with him. But he would not accept me as anything but his child who should in all good sense let him run his life. He never outgrew my childhood and this contradiction always showed in his behavior.

Katherine Siswick-Clark:

Thank you Pradeep for sharing your insights. I agree that there are so many contradictions. I think parents want their children to be free thinkers, independent, confident and self assured when they are older, but as children the opposite!!! Partly because its easier to deal with a child who listens and accepts things, and the whole 'do as I say not as I do' idea, and also because that's often how they were brought up. Its can be a challenge to nurture those desired qualities in children and maintain balance as its the unknown for many, but I think parents are changing the way they respond to their children and seeing the need to foster high self esteem, confidence, independent thought and problem solving, The world is definitely evolving

Ana Prpic:

Pradeep, I think there is always something good in everything, no matter how bad it is (or it seems). I have a feeling you learnt a lesson, so to speak, and you won't, or you will try not to, make the same mistakes with your kids. But, that doesn't mean you won't make some new ones :)

Pradeep Pk Maheshwari: My father was always there for me and wanted to do the best he understood to be good. But he was hampered by being the Lord in a rich feudal joint family and he simply did not know how to communicate - there was never any real need. Whatever he wanted, he got done; whatever he said, nobody ever questioned him – at least aloud. It was one way - everything fine but no conversation or sharing.

Steve Lochmueller:

Unfortunately it's not just family structures such as the one you described that create that type of interaction between child and parent. The divorce rate in the United States is off the chart, creating generation after generation of parentless children. I refer to parentless children as those raised by a single parent. Where you describe a controlling father without communication skills, I suffered through a non-existent father figure (as is the case for many men raised by their mother because of divorce). Many of the important life lessons are lost due to this dynamic, and create even more problems when these men have children of their own. I certainly lacked some important skills in raising children because I only had half of the process taught to me. I had to learn on the fly, so to speak, while raising my sons, so I am as guilty as your father in that respect. I found myself at times making statements similar to "because I said so" to my children. I am not proud of this, but without the knowledge being passed down from my father, I like to think I did the best I could. That is not to suggest that my father would have been able to pass along some type of universal knowledge for raising children, but I would have been able to process his actions and lessons towards me and used that to decide how I should teach my sons. The point is that each time a son (future father) is required to learn on their own it reverses the process of progression in raising children.

Pradeep Pk Maheshwari:

I agree with you here. This is why I raised this question on my personal page:

Pl give yr view on: I have been rather concerned but now more than just worried about the regular news of students committing suicides because they are afraid of not doing well and social pressures. But I feel there is something here that goes a lot deeper. I wish to study this subject a little more in depth. There is also the subject of young people in schools going berserk and shooting etc.

Topic No 6

The older little ones

I saw this cartoon where the young lady is telling her friends how she never thought she would end up with two kids, one little one and one big one – her husband – and the fact that all the self-help books are only on the subject of little ones. Well, I am not writing a book here but I am definitely willing to share some of my thoughts.

Some time back, I took a gift box of toffees to my sister and while giving it to her I said – here is something for your three children; she has only 2 daughters. It took her second but she caught on that the third child I was referring to was her husband. And she agreed. So I suppose the problem is rather more universal and far flung than one would imagine.

Let us take one problem at a time.

1) He thinks he is the master/lord and the grown up around there.
My view would be that is how you stringed him along and now you will have to live with it. You can always use your tears to control the situation if it is going out of hand. But if you think you can do much about changing the situation than you are living an illusion. Seriously speaking I would advise you to leave the subject of trying to change him alone.

2) She thinks she runs/owns the place.
She literally does. You should have thought of it before you put her up on that pedestal in your eagerness to put that the ring on her finger. You knew all along that your independence was at stake and you would now be living under her rule. It was acceptable when courting; now grin and bear it. Just change your own mindset and if you have to look for another place to keep your shaving brush, just do it.

3) Can we discuss this like mature adults?
No we can't for the obvious fact that we are not mature adults. Mature adults do not go around carrying their heart on one sleeve, their egos on the other and their mobile phones tightly clamped in their hands. Then, most adults never discuss. They accuse outright. This cannot augur well by any standard.

104

4) Whose house is it anyway?

Peace descends on all households once this question is firmly resolved. Most couples do not even know that most of the problems of their life together are stemming from this question at the back of their minds. And the children know for sure that it belongs to them; thereby only compounding the intricacy of the problem. Women say that they were brought in by marriage and why would any man would do that if he did not want to let her feel so? She is right. Most men think that because they are earning members, all rights are theirs. I am on the side of women here; this is the most stupid thought a man can have. And if the woman is the earning member then it is best if the man thought of himself as the vassal in the equation.

5) On the question of habits.

Most habits are there to stay. Both the partners have picked them up on their growing up saga and I see not how they will change now. He leaves used glasses everywhere with rings all over the place which makes the woman livid. She uses his towel and he goes all red. These problems are of their own making. They need to be taken with a pinch of salt.

When we first get married we want to be entwined. But sooner or later the novelty wears off and then we want our private space back. I wonder if there is any going back.

My personal experience is that we are in it for the duration. Men should try to create small corners for themselves in their homes without making it too obvious that they are doing so. Hide important things if needed.

Most women who move things around do not realize the frustration and time lost in looking for things. Small things which most often, as they have been moved by another person cannot be found without the other's help anyway. Women on the other hand should be ready for being treated as the happy partner, whatever happens: like he bringing in two of his friends for dinner and she not properly made up. Most women may complain on how is she to provide for two sudden guests; but the truth is that this does not bother her at all. She could cook up something with one hand tied behind her back. But being caught unprepared with her hair in disarray is something else; she cannot ever forgive that. Men need to understand these fine points.

6) Shall we ever learn?

Come on, wake up. The learning process stopped long ago. We are now an evolved couple – are we not? That we are continuously getting into each other's hair because "I know best and refuse to shift my stance" is another matter. Anyone can see that I am changing and adjusting; if only I could say the same for my partner!

7) Illness and babyism.

When it comes to illness like sore throats and a slight fever or even a little pain, men show their real selves. They have learnt from early on that when they are sick they get the most attention. Now I firmly blame the women for this. Unfortunately what the mothers sow has to be reaped by the wives. But then men have no role in this fiasco and should not be blamed!

Some comments by friends:

Edward Stanulevich IV:

I have noticed that women do not seem to understand that a man needs his space. They tend to take this as rejection. It is not. Women tend to deal with stress and emotions by being in a group and doing whatever secret girl things they do. Men deal with stress and emotions by being alone, often thinking the problem out.

Men focus in on problem solving, were as women focus in on the feeling of the situation.

Both I and my wife understand this. She gives me all the space I need, when I need it. I give her the best emotional outlet I can. I am still working on listening without trying to fix the problem, but she is helping me with this. I just do not fully understand getting upset at a situation and not doing something about it.

But then, men and women deal with this in very different ways.

Ana Prpic:

Pradeep my dear friend, pity there ain't no women around to comment...

I don't dare any more. :D

Again, I don't get if this > Anyone can see that I am changing and adjusting; if only I could say the same for my partner!< and

> But then men have no role in this fiasco and should not be blamed!<

is sarcastic, ironic or you truly mean it?

I can understand the need to create a small corner for yourself in your home, and the need to be left alone when dealing with a problem, I do it too. There's only one friend who I talk to when dealing with any kind of bad situation, I like her rational, objective perspective. But, hanging around other women (and being one) I dare say this, most women want little signs of appreciation and affection, want their partners to listen, but listen with honest attention. And if you truly believe that men should not be blamed for whatever part in raising the kids, my opinion is that, well, you're simply wrong. Raising children together, by both partners, gives them responsibility, blame and appreciation.

Pradeep Pk Maheshwari:

Let's discuss your comments Ana.

Again, I don't get if this > Anyone can see that I am changing and adjusting; if only I could say the same for my partner!<

Whenever we discuss change, we humans tend to eulogise our own selves and find the faults in others. This is our general tendency. Ask any Marriage Counselor about how this translates in marriages.

It is all a matter of giving space to each other. When we do this we see the other better, then appreciation follows and affection as a matter of course. I read somewhere a quote which goes something like this: Marriage is like a wood fire. To have a good fire the logs have to be together but with a little space between them to burn properly.

Mostly we end up taking each other for granted.

And in the above I am quoting for all relationships.

and

> But then men have no role in this fiasco and should not be blamed!<

is sarcastic, ironic or you truly mean it?

Well, there is of course some deep truth embedded here but the sharp tone may find women crying foul. The tone is a little sarcastic to make proper impact. But it is based on the fact; mainly that humanity sees nursing as something of a woman's role. I am only basing it on this although as intelligent people we know that it is not true.

But generally speaking, it is the women/mothers who do the pampering, especially when boys are sick. They like this and expect the same even when they are doddering well into their 90s.

These lines of yours:

And if you truly believe that men should not be blamed for whatever part in raising the kids, my opinion is that, well, you're simply wrong. Raising children together, by both partners, gives them responsibility, blame and appreciation.

Here you have got things a little wrong. My statement was strictly on the question of babyism in sickness. You cannot expand it the way you have done to include the entire gamut of parenting.

Though, it is best to try and go behind the words and understand the underlying concepts in play than focusing purely on the words like lawyers would do in court.

Ooi Kok Wan:

From my point of view, fault is something that is beautiful.. wonderful.. it shows how imperfect we are...

If we truly understand this.. we can understand about ourselves.. and also our partners..

No one is perfect, not your partner.. not even ourselves.. to love someone, it actually means to understand and accept your partner and "yourself" too..

*****

A teacher draws a small dot on the big white board with a small marker pen.. she asks: "what is this?"

The pupils all answer quickly: "A black dot."

The teacher laughs and says: "This is a big white board."

*****

A black dot is so small but when it was placed on the big white board, you can really understand how big the white board that you have... is ^^

If we just like to pick on small things.. and we might end up losing the big picture.. >.<

I am still single.. T.T

But I learn this from my parents... although they are not happily married.. but they teach me a lesson that hard for people to understand.. ^^

My pass is nothing to be sad or ashamed of.. it is just a learning curve if you can understand "life"..

My parents is "indirectly the best teacher" I or anyone can ever had.. >.<

The small dot is my parents marriage.. the big white board is actually what I have learned or other people can understand from this pass of mine.. ^^

Edward Stanulevich IV

"I dare say this, most women want little signs of appreciation and affection, want their partners to listen, but listen with honest attention."

Yep.

I still like the old "it takes a village to raise a child" idea.

Thanks Ooi, I will spend some time meditating on that black dot thing.

Pradeep Maheshwari:

I learned a lot from my parents by observing them. And of course observing other parents around me because I had to live time with my uncles. In India we had the benefit of joint families. I definitely saw the things that were grating on everybody's nerves and made me question – why are they so? I read all the books on psychology I could find and all the books written by spiritual masters that I could lay my hands on.

I resolved to not marry until I was, at least in my own thoughts, ready to take on the responsibility of another person in my life.

And when I did marry, another universe unfolded. And I realised how un-ready I was. The process of change and learning actually started at this stage because I was ready to listen and see myself through my partner's eyes.

Dave Shapiro:

From Kahlil Girbran: But let there be spaces in your togetherness and let the heavens dance between you. Love one another, but make not a bond of love. Fill each others cup but do not drink from just one cup......

Amir Mourad:

If two individuals involved in a relationship are naturally in harmony within themselves at the level of consciousness, the relationship takes care of itself without even any effort on one's own part. Because what we call relationship is just an interaction between certain minds functioning within a certain inner state. The same formula applies in relationship beyond just two people, when you extend it outwards to include the whole society. The social conditions that are experienced are a direct reflection of the average state of consciousness of the average individual.

But the reason why there is so much friction often in relationships is simply because very few people understand how to become involved without creating all kinds of rules, regulations, conditions, and barriers. Because people live out of a deep lust for security, they have to create these barriers around everything in life; it even becomes projected into the relationship. Why should one function any differently in a relationship than as one functions in the rest of one's life? It is not the kind of condition of a Sunday church Christian or a religious dogmatic who enters into the temple as one person, and immediately exits to return to his old usual patterns. If you walk into a space which you think is sacred carrying all of the accumulated garbage, it will remain in the temple, and it will remain upon leaving the temple because no deeper awareness has occurred.

You cannot separate your involvement with another from the rest of life. Everything in life is interconnected and all areas are influencing the other areas in a very complex way. That is why, for one who lives with awareness, there is a certain art and science of living. He no longer looks at his life in isolated fragments, but holistically, with an understanding of how every part of the mechanism of a machine contributes to the functioning of the whole structure.

Do not enter relationship carrying all of the psychological projections within you, because one will knowingly or unknowingly contaminate the relationship with those projections. Those projections may appear beautiful, or they may appear not so beautiful, but it makes no difference. A projection is a projection, you can neither see yourself clearly, nor the other person. You look at your wife or your girlfriend with the idea already programmed that she is one's wife or girlfriend, but you never want to see the person as a whole, without the images one has created about the person.

If you cannot see yourself clearly, how can you expect to see anything else clearly? It is a simple formula. Whatever you are projecting onto the outside world is none other than your own very qualities which you are carrying within yourself.

Pradeep Pk Maheshwari:

You have explained it well Mourad. The first thing we were taught was to become our own witness: To BE and then also to stand aside and look at ourselves as a "third party". This gives us objectivity and the ability to see things in us and around us dispassionately, without the involvement of the ego and the subconscious.

In this condition the higher mind is using every relationship and situation to learn and educate oneself. It sees things clearly. Both the positive attributes and the negative and one can then charter one's course with ease; always in control. All that happens is then always our own fault and we then work on our faults to become a better person, often helping others too in the process.

This results in a lot of harmonious happenings.

Comment by George Shepherd

Much food for thought. The one paragraph that hits close to home with me is number 2). You are right Pradeep, I can't change what I created, but I can - hopefully - change my mindset.

Comment by Steve MacDowall

Number 2 hit me also - not only our mind set but how we talk and interact can really give good feedback without telling someone something.

Interesting thoughts - Beverly and I work as one when it comes to our home and family - She is the doer and I am the dreamer - it is good to get our rolls down as to what the other one thinks of us. I like to cook; she likes horses, we both like gardening. I love to read; she love to watch movies. I like to spend money; she loves to save. I love my classical music; she likes light rock and instrumental stuff. We both love to be around one another most of the time. The one place we have to work on is in the kitchen. - a few thoughts from my side.

Topic No 7

On the concept of Conflict and Competition.

Pradeep Pk Maheshwari Had there been no conflict, we would not take the trouble to see ourselves as we are or even think of better things. We would be totally complacent. Competition is friendly conflict; necessary to goad the humans into achieving something greater.

Divyaa Kummar

Conflict is not actually the conflict of opposition/ disagreement as we usually take it to be- it is the very force underlying existence- its physics- its what allows anything to birth...w/o it nothing could be...

Dave Shapiro:

Hey Pradeep..how about a game of chess or go????

Pradeep Pk Maheshwari:

Chess was my game and I was even good at it. I suppose I could give a good fight still. Can't find players (or anyone for that matter. Shutting off the phone makes them gasp for air) anymore who could sit still for an hour or two

117

Dave Shapiro

I still sit for hours......try living in Alaska in the winter...there's nothing else to do after you walk the dogs and snow plow the driveway for the 40th time...

Pradeep Pk Maheshwari

I meant willingly, totally engrossed in what they are doing or just enjoying being alone. Hope you are not making a virtue out of a necessity. Secretly between you and me, I would.

Dave Shapiro

Not sure about that...I really enjoy my alone time but am not lonely....my virtues are few but the ones I have I do well...

Pradeep Pk Maheshwari

Intelligent, talented and capable people are never lonely. So your statement proves what I knew about you all along.

Janelle Portelli

118

Competition for me with others is not my forte...unless it is really not serious. I love sing star karaoke great if I'm not too shy....I compete with myself though everyday to become more each day in spite of all my trials, tribulations and shortcomings.....I try and make it a friendly conflict by learning to be kind to oneself as I am to others... yes as you say become something greater... like the process of alchemy I imagine it as akin to, whatever your playing field...I rather try and find an equal ground with people though I struggle for all of us to see equality, this can be competitive yes but its tiring...and yes alone time and rest is needed to ensure one does not feel lonely in times of solitude or gregariousness.

Pradeep Pk Maheshwari

Janelle, that is the perfect attitude. Why should we compete with others? We are what we are and when we are honest and sincere with ourselves we are the best judge. The principal question is: Are we happy and satisfied with ourselves or we feel there is space for improvement?

Janelle Portelli:

I get happy for awhile though then I seek further...not always more knowledge or enlightenment but even to make things simpler sometimes..... I always strive for improvement but I can't do it all day...if u don't sit back n smell a few roses...what would be the point..... Happiness is a mindset that I try to maintain. I do the best I can; emotions follow...when I'm successful...which I do at times. I try to learn.....that's as honest as I can put it I think....

119

Gro Viste

I wish I could write in my own language. But anyway.... Conflicts can of course be both positive and negative, depending on the issue, I think. Conflicts that lead to war and killing of innocent people are in my opinion never a good thing. But conflict that opens up to more understanding and knowledge between us is a good thing. In reality we don't know how life without small or large conflicts would be like. There are always wars going on, - between countries or people. Could be interesting and nice to live a life in peace and see how that is. I know that I am more healthy and happy when our family and friends are in peace. I think it is important to show your face and talk about your needs so people can see you and better understand you. Very important is to understand that we all are unique. There is a phrase going like this: "There is only one success - to spend your life in your own way" .... but I will add something important: ....."if it does not hurt somebody". (and in this there could be a conflict...) So there we go..... and I hope in peace ▢

Janelle Portelli

Gro, yes, I guess its all about perspective yes it is true so much conflict and competition in the world....I try make the best and most peaceful out of what comes into my life...and the bit at the end... yes I know the paradox you are speaking of.........we can only strive for peace and balance in this with best intentions....accidents happen, I guess....we all get a bit bumped and bruised a little.......

Pradeep Pk Maheshwari

Gro What you say is correct but you are expanding the comment of Competition and Conflict to war. Here we were focusing more on the personal day to day conflicts and personal attitudes & self improvement.

Pradeep Pk Maheshwari

Janelle, don't be in a hurry. This process lasts a life time and as we believe here in India, goes on and on in many lives till we arrive back to the core of our Divine being.

Kokayi Ufanifu

For small minds competition may be the answer, but for people who understand LOVE = cooperation, sharing, and caring we don't need that kind of Win-Lose way of living!

Janelle Portelli

I know this my friend. Well I feel it is like it is...perhaps personal experience has given me glimpses of this truth some of us find..... I have cultivated a lot of patience though with myself... this is the greatest

121

struggle with patience of all…. although perhaps this lifetime I decided to experience things at this time through the filter of a 29 year old girl….. I know I'm still young so I'm cool with it…but thank you are right though…..evolving is like a garden that takes a long time to become really beautiful and self-sustaining… I guess that's a way of describing it….. win-win is possible…. if we try!!!! Perhaps… I like to hope anyway!!!

Ceferino Díaz:

 It is typical of a narcissist culture in which talent is undervalued and fame and glamour is at the top. To see a musician in a subway for free is not glamorous, it does not add any social status to the musician nor to the audience; to pay $100.00 to see a musician in a theatre gives social status, it is glamorous.

Pradeep Pk Maheshwari:

Too true. It is such a perverted situation. People don't do things because their true persona wants it. Everything is calculated TO CREATE AN IMPRESSION. We live to fit-in, join-the-right n proper-club: To be seen and appreciated- finally our own well being and earning depend on being seen and appreciated with those who have money because in the final analysis they are the ones who will help us pay the bills.

Dave Shapiro

On another tangent, how many of us compete with the clock?

Pradeep Pk Maheshwari

Yes. This instrument has a most devilish hold on us. But it does help us to synchronise and work together without wasting each other's time.

Dave Shapiro: Agreed and it is how we use the time we have that matters the most. Does it control us or do we use it as the stream flows......

Topic No 8

On Homework from School

Homework set by teachers for the child seems to be a very important aspect of schooling, at least in India. They start with kindergarten. There is always something that has to be practiced to make perfect. I have been a teacher and I must say I understand these feelings by the teachers that there is so much to learn and they wish to impart it all to their wards in one go with 100% accuracy and totality if possible. But is that wise?

123

I had to teach myself to be patient and not be in a hurry to push the students to do more and more. For many reasons, one of them being the basic character make-up of every child; all children are not made the same way and there are bound to be some who cannot take any pushing at all. Then, most children flower at different speeds and we must respect this factor.

My child is not even five, and the teachers are asking us to spend time to make the child finish homework that they have given. Most of the teachers and educationists agree that the program is far too huge for children to assimilate but as the authorities/experts and powers to be have decided, the program has to be followed. The parents are being roped in to back this need. The sad aspect is that most parents do not see anything amiss and rather go in the direction of asking the schools to do more.

Now for somebody running a school, of course the program is important. Rather from the vantage point of his position, nothing else matters. He has to push the envelop that he has been entrusted with; that is what he is there for. His job and life depend upon it. Then is the child of no importance?

Recently I came across a book Rules of Parenting by Richard Templar. It was lying there in somebody's house and I opened it at random and the page opened at the heading:

Parents should not become teachers.

The author puts out this argument that teaching is best left to teachers in schools and parents need to be parents only. The stress and phobias of the school should remain in school and should not be allowed to get extended to the home.

Do not management experts advise people to leave their work stress at the office and not carry it home; so why this advice is not being followed when children are being managed?

I fully agree about this. Let us not give the child the feeling from the age of 4 that life is a chore. I have seen children under the load to keep their elders happy get into the habit of trying to somehow satisfy and fool their elders rather think of their own personal enhancement. We are putting them into wrong attitudes of hiding, cheating, lying and taking short-cuts. Rather our duty lies in making him realize that life is an adventure and learning makes it more fun. People who understand the "How"s and "Why"s are better tuned to get the maximum out of it. For eventually there is also this need to become a proper member of society in which education and training is responsible to get positions of authority and more control of one's own life.

I would rather teach my child to tie his laces, lay the table, make his bed and clean-up after he is done than make him write abc. I understand the need for the child to do his homework but I will NOT push him to it as an extension of his school. Let there be no two thoughts or doubts on this score. I am the child's parent and the school should not take me for granted that I will become an unpaid teacher for them. Let them reduce the workload or increase the class work time or whatever they can think of.

Let's have an understanding. The school takes care of the child's IQ and we parents take care of his EQ. Agreed?

The home is a sanctuary. This is the place where the child comes after being buffeted by the winds of the world outside his door. The parents are the pillars he holds on to. Let us be careful to maintain this position. The parents should help, assist and support. Listen to the child and be there for him. Any parent who just stands there with a stick in his hand as a trainer & as an extension of the bad horrible world of the authorities from the outside the child's door is inviting disaster.

If the news and spate of incidences of suicides, running-aways and shootings has not opened our eyes, I wonder what will.

In my personal case, what I did was to create an atmosphere where the child would feel like wanting to sit down and do his work. Right from the time she was a baby. I would hold her in my arm and work with the other on my computer. I have made it a point to sit down at my work table at regular times and the child has learnt that I do not like to be disturbed at this time because I work with focus and undivided attention to what I am doing and I would do other things in the house only when I have finished my work. This was step one. An atmosphere and culture was created and the child was made to absorb this with proper regularity. Now that the child is big enough, I have put a table alongside mine and which gives the child his own space. Now I am encouraging my child to come and sit by me and do his work without being goaded or tormented or shouted at. Once this becomes a trend and habit, this will be part of his character for the rest of his waking life and I am sure will stand him in good stead.

I see in many households (Rather more than less) that the parents do not maintain any kind of discipline or atmosphere of study or work but expect the child to do so. This is asking for the moon.

And for the school authorities I have this message. Be kinder and softer. Reduce the stress and work load. The learning process does not stop or exist only within school walls. Don't try to make the child into a Master by the time he has finished with you.

Siddhartha wrote back:

Great words PK. I fully subscribe to your views. Time and again, parents fall into a classical trap of chasing the child to do tasks at the cost of their normal childhood. Some parents argue that making a child competitive is the only thing that matters. Thought leaders have written that - as recent as day before by eminent people like R Gopalakrishnan of Tata Sons - several people with high IQ suffer from mid career crisis due to lack of appreciation of EQ. Most parents are concerned about the IQ bit, little realising the eventual damage. You have rightly raised more fundamental point about all round development including self discipline, and action focus, helpfulness, all of which does not get picked up and rewarded by our education system. I am glad that you have chosen to share your concern and opted to be the change.

Rene Rayson:

Wow sounds like you were are a great teacher when you worked in school and sounds like you are a very good teacher and parent at home. I must agree with your statement sir fully you have my full respect for your writing and view.

Globbler:

That's a very interesting perspective on child education, Pradeep! Thank you for sharing. I would like to add that schools should involve global studies in the curriculum and educate our future generations of the importance of understanding and collaborating with other cultures, compassion, tolerance, love and peace.

Kelvin Qiu:

In early years, our school had a rush in raising the amount of "knowledge" in student. Parent here are still shocked over what they used to learn in secondary education is being pushed into primary education. Parents who are well educated themselves can barely cope with the homework of their children.

Are we producing "robot" students who do well academically vs. rest of world at the expense of being "all rounder" (street smart). Now there is interest to bring back more field trips and other activities, school should not be all about classroom learning, it makes us square and uncreative.

Despite Asia producing the most number of engineers in the world, our ability to produce totally new products are lacking. We are unable to get out of the box; I hope our future generation would be taught creative skills, not just stuffed with knowledge.

And yes the home is where the children gain their traits, "it runs in the family", parent are the role model of kids. Good parenting requires effort. but as more families become duel income families, kids spend more and more time alone, they are force to develop their social behavior on their own...

Meenam Malhotra:

Some hours spent per day are sufficient for a child's intellectual and academic growth. rest of the day is to be divided into the child's physical, emotional, social, creative, spirit growth,...whether at school or at home or both...the formula devised is one to one, there can be no generalisations. It depends on what the parents are like and the family environment. However, I agree that example is the best teacher, and parents and / or teachers must practice what they teach/ preach.

Dave Shapiro:

As long as homework is seen as a chore the kids will turn away. With the advent of computers ...hopefully the assignments will become more fun and interesting but the parents and teachers will have to provide positive motivation and caring and most important...creativity and desire to want to learn...

From: "Mind Management™"

mindmanagement@gmail.com......To: "PK"

130

s164gk1@yahoo.com.......Well articulated Pradeep :-)

Simrin Haz:

Mr Maheshwari what do you do, when as a parent, the competition is so tough for your ward to get into the field that they aspire to do so? They have to deliver; the schools have to deliver hence the HOMEWORK!

Pradeep Pk Maheshwari The question is: Is homework the only route? A secondary question is: Is the curriculum being followed correct/appropriate/useful/wise?

Anu Arundhathi:

Dear PK, I have been through all this again and again as a teacher as well as a parent and kind of given up after many disappointments and heart breaks. The only answer I found most of the time is that all this is happening due to population explosion and too much competition in our country. People are willing to do anything to survive here at any condition. No one complains, no one tries to find any alternative ways ...in fact no one even thinks...

Do you have hope that you can do something?

Regards:~Anu .

Pradeep Pk Maheshwari

Frankly; NO. I gave up teaching and my associations with many schools here as a trainer for teachers because of the conditions you mention.

But there is a little awakening in some parents - still a minority. My dream was to find a school to run so that I could direct and shape the destinies of at least some kids. But the Universe is not handing me out even a small broken bone. I hope I can at least do something for my daughter.

Anu Arundhathi :

I totally understand your anxiety and your pain as I been through this for my daughter and still going through....As caring parents we try and do a lot to give children a perfect world. But we are facing a world which is very messed up...In my opinion some things are getting worse everyday...I have been and I still keep teaching her to face all this and survive. Even I am struggling for my survival due to the current scenario. All the best for your attempts and wish you all the success!

 Pradeep Pk Maheshwari :

Well we are two from the same ship at least.

Comment by Steve MacDowall

> My children are 25, 28 and 31. The first two started their schooling in Ontario and when we moved to New Brunswick the third child started to get into the halls of learning. We started to teach our children when they were very young. We even put away the TV so we would have more time to play with them and to do things

together like reading. Learning starts early and it really never ends. There are many different types of learning, school is but one and it's time should not flow into other time periods where the child should be with the family. If a child is at school for, let's say, 6 hours a day, then that should be enough to lean, practice, and evaluate what they are learning. If, as they do these days, go beyond that time line, then the system is not set up properly. Language, (reading and writing along with grammar should be on top) Math's, and people skills next – then add in history, geography etc. Most studies show that the average student has a very low level of communication skills along with math. It's not by adding more time to the child's school education; it is the system of leaning, teaching and communicating that must be addressed and changed. Let kids be kids

Cea Weaver:

People can [easily] be pushed too hard... and then they may lose all interest... the middle way is good :)

Teya Slo :

Dear Pradeep, this is perfectly written! I agree every child is unique and the school system wants to be fast and successful in its own way, many times forgetting the meaning of humanity. I believe that parents have to be attentive about what is going on in a school and at the same time I think that they should not be involved too much in the whole school atmosphere. I think that a school belongs to the children and they can share it with their parents - inviting them into it by speaking about it or on school celebrations etc. All the rest of the time a child should develop his own independency in the middle of the class by himself, that's growing, too. Spending quality time with parents can be put anywhere else - not right in the school, again. It's the truth that this two fields are being mixed these days, for few special occasions can be fine, but not on so many different school projects or later too many home works, I totally agree (sincere congrats for the wonderful discipline attitude passing to a child!). For the IQ and EQ I think it could be thought anywhere all the time - we are mirrors, students and teachers to each other anyplace, anytime. What's the title of the book you mentioned, please? Thank You for the great post, I loved to read it. Nice regards and best wishes!

Topic No 9

IN THE REALM OF WORDS

I started a discussion on my FB group – "Sufi Speaks" and the exchanges that came forth are worth noting so I am sharing them with you here:

Pradeep Pk Maheshwari **When we quote other greats, are we sharing our joy of discovery or showing off that we appreciate the point of view and could be considered equally great?**

Vishwajeet : Sometimes deep inside you want to say, express something, some emotion and are not getting the right kind of words, then if you happen to see certain quote which appeals to you and your heart resonates with it, you feel like sharing it with your friends too.

Phalgun Desai: For me it is sharing the joy of discovering great words spoken by enlightened souls. Knowledge of this kind has to be shared.

Janet Bennison :   Or ? I am thinking both the joy of discovery & an appreciation of that person's point of view. From my personal point of view this does not endow me with 'greatness'.

Jimmy K. Mody : When we quote Great people, perhaps sometimes we are sharing our discoveries in order to project ourselves as great/special. Sometimes, therefore, both could be simultaneous.

Divyaa Kummar: Sometimes it's just that someone has 'said' it before us! Or better than us! So we use the quote! Sometimes yes it's like a deep recognition of what is within but not expressed/expressible; sometimes it's that Zen kwatz! Something that just hits home and thus the simplest way of sharing-is... thru it directly!

Pradeep Pk Maheshwari **The question that follows: Why are some people always using the route of "quotes" to voice their thoughts and feelings? Perhaps because this way they eliminate any discussions and argument as the quotes are from well established personas?!**

Divyaa Kummar : Yet I do not make 'not using quotes' into some binding either... if a quote pops up in my reaching out/expression I allow it to... but more to coalesce it all ...in words which do justice more than mine...!

But yes I must confess I have experienced (somewhat to my amused chagrin) that a quote from a renowned master somehow makes what I have expressed more sacrosanct!!!! It's strange how many a time when people are hearing/reading you they are not really 'listening'/open... as much as 'agreeing or disagreeing...!!! And to those specially, the quote from a master makes it more easy to agree with ;-)) ! But it's ok! Each to their own! But yes I prefer to write ...and read...people's own expressions rather than only through quotes-however bingo they may be!

Richard Schooping : When we resonate with an energy it is then that energy that we naturally express. When we strike a bell that is attuned to

136

certain frequency, all bells at that frequency vibrate, or we may say all others share the same quotes.

Margie Myers-Yanes : Generally when I post a quote it's something that inspired me, stirred my soul and I pass it along.

Pradeep Pk Maheshwari Yes there is this joy of discovery and then collecting for later reference and reminding us. I collect them and do like to pass on hoping others would enjoy them too - like a good joke.

Pradeep Pk Maheshwari on QUOTES. **One question no one has touched upon. Why are we so inclined to pass on our excitement to just about anybody OR showing the way to others?**

Suresh C Sharma Sharing is a joy: Joy is our nature.

Pradeep Pk Maheshwari : Real sharing is always a joy. It becomes problem when it is a calculated giving. Very few of us give without having calculated some benefit in any deal - however insignificant.

Gro Viste : It is the receiver who values the gift...

A calculated giver is a person in need.... let us help him ▯

Richard Schooping : The Sun in its joy-of-being radiates, and we now say that all benefit from this light. But ask yourself, does the Sun think about who or what is in its radiance? I propose no, as its perpetual joy "is" in its being the Sun. If the Sun thought about these things it would be a mere blinking strobe light and not the Sun seeing that its awareness would be continually shifting from mind to stillness.

We know that the Sun is a realized being through its expressed constancy of love. So it is the ego that decides its relationship with the Sun, and not the Sun, and therein is the shift in understanding.

Another reader: I am fed up with the negative games we play.

Pradeep Pk Maheshwari : Being fed up is a negative thing too. You cannot allow yourself to be fed up. The "muck" is there and if we ignore it, we give it power to grow.

.

"Words are not a good medium in the first place. Then there are literal and figurative meanings + idioms to boot; enough to make a vanilla cake become chocolate with a swish of the pen. Things get and are wilfully embellished in the telling. When people do not understand a quote themselves, they reword it to suit their own comprehension levels. Over time things get worse or totally changed & twisted/manipulated into something totally else."

Unfortunately there is a high element of self-centeredness and cleverness in HUMANs to be good transferors of messages with words.

We started with grunts and evolved into the complex language of today. Without words we would not have even got started. Words can be fun and keep us busy and involved. Like the TV. So we eventually need to evolve to the next step and see the frontage as well as go behind the words where a single word can help your intuitive side open a whole window and see a whole vast picture without the help of the interpreting and judging mind.

Topic No 10

Listen and Be Damned.

I am tired of being told that to live a more efficient life I need to become a good listener. Open any book on self development, spiritual emancipation, marriage counselling or management science and the same advice glares at you from all sides. All the glitches are from poor listening if there is any listening in the first place. Not a single writer, philosopher or guru ever mentions the other side of the picture.

Tell me how will listening help? I am here to make my life easy; not yours. If I listen, I put myself in the unedifying position of wanting to better myself and do a good job. This would in turn bring in appreciation and then everybody would be gunning for me to do more. No sir! I just wish to bide my time and would like a lot of margin to hedge my bets. I love people with poor language abilities and even poorer interpersonal behaviour patterns. In this situation I am always able to find excuses and faults enough to cover my intentions of not wanting to do anything in the first place.

I sincerely have not understood how listening could be of help to me. I live in my very private cocoon; perfectly smug in my little comfortable corner. I am aware of my faults and till date I have been covering them up quite well; or at least I think so. From what I can see, listening can only bring me a host of complications. I can site many examples. I would rather spend my time arguing it out (what would politely be called discussion) than really going about doing wonderfully all that I am capable of doing and gather praises.

My wife asks me to put out the garbage. But as she likes to talk long distance with her face mostly in the opposite direction with her face stuck inside some pot or shelf, it gives me the perfect excuse to feign as if I never heard anything and ignore the situation, hoping that she would do the job herself. If I am caught out there would be enough arguments up my sleeve to at least put up a show of indignation. You see I simply cannot make it easy for her. If I did so, the number of jobs that I would end up doing would only grow in number. Believe me, I am better off with my reputation of being absent-minded, partly deaf or weak in the head or whatever.

In the office, I always put up a good show of listening while my mind is flitting all over the globe. It is a good thing they can't see my thoughts. Last evening I was called in by my boss. He wanted me to receive a company head at the airport; a job he was slated to be doing himself. Now I definitely do not appreciate being ploughed into this kind of secretarial duties. So I said nothing then, but an hour before the flight, I rang up the boss to tell him that I was 40 kms away on another job I had been assigned and docilely started asking him for advice on how to complete the job to his entire satisfaction. Now he was in a fix. Here I was asking for advice while he wanted to be angry and ask me why I was not on the way to the airport. Finally he did ask the question. I had already rehearsed my answer. So I showed surprise and replied that was it not in the morning that I was supposed to go to the airport. The boss fumed and knew that he been outfoxed and went himself eventually. So you see!

Now I am no junior either but my boss is one step ahead of me and does not let me forget it. He tries to ply me with work that he should be doing himself. My plate is already full and he knows it. So what; that does not stop him. Now you would readily have reckoned, the whole of my existence is to slip out of sticky situations. If I listened it would be the end of me.

The truth of the matter is that humanity does not want to listen. We live in a very self-cantered world and are content to be there. Listening opens us to betterment and that is not really desired. What would happen to our personal agendas that in the normal course we dare not expose to others? Listening allows seeds to be sowed in the heart which will, of course, grow and upset the status quo no end.

Here I have just brushed the subject as far as we see in our daily existences. The truth is that NOT listening is the norm; even in other more truthful environments like spirituality, ashrams and religious societies. Life is lived like a charade with many lies being promoted and practiced because it suits everybody. I look at my own and the life of others around me. Believe me I am not really surprised. I don't see anyone achieving their human aims by playing clean and fair. Lies, even evident lies are vehemently promoted and lapped up. To believe me all you need is to see some of the adverts on the TV, some of the truths propagated by religious leaders, some of the principles of schooling in practice, most of the medical principles advanced and found wanting and continued nevertheless.

Listening means peeping in corners we are really not keen on. It then insists that attention be paid, being alert and aware. Who in the name of heaven really wants all that? I am appalled at the idea that my amour proper will have to take a back seat. This won't do at all. Listening would mean throwing the science of keeping appearances in the dustbin and revealing ourselves in all our insincere nakedness to the world. Sorry this is not acceptable and that is that!

I am here to fulfil my selfish ends and am not averse to join in the drama. Once I have made my pile that will allow me to live out my life to my wishes, who would care about listening anyway?

Edward Stanulevich IV:

"My wife asks me to put out the garbage. But as she likes to talk long distance with her face mostly in the opposite direction with her face stuck inside some pot or shelf"

Now I really am worried that we have the same wife...

As for listening, I enjoy listening, most of the time. Helps keep me grounded, cantered and present.

Pradeep Pk Maheshwari:

Now this is worrying.....one is bad enough. But then I wonder if cloning has been taking place behind our backs. Shall we band together and create a society?

Ana Prpic:

Where are the girls on this board so that we can exchange experiences about husbands and boyfriends?

Pradeep, are you a bit sarcastic about listening? Otherwise I'm going to seriously question my knowledge of English language.

Edward Stanulevich IV:

Ana, I live in Alabama. Your English is better than most of the Americans here.

Really, they speak a dialect called "Southern" that took me 3 months to understand. I was born and raised in the USA!

His posts are just a little different in their perspectives.

Pradeep Pk Maheshwari

When you have seen life properly you tend to see the jokes. Some may call it sarcasm. Anyway sarcasm is something with a sadistic bite in it. My aim was to open minds to the other side's view.

Dave Shapiro:

Cosmic jokes are like that I think....How can we look around and not laugh and cry...two sides of the same things..

David Flynn:

I'm from Oz and I understood.

Ana Prpic:

Pradeep, I didn't mean to imply you were sadistic at all. I don't see you that way, nor the sarcasm in general. You just don't strike me as a person who'd say > I am here to fulfil my selfish ends <

Pradeep Pk Maheshwari:

You see Ana, I write what I "see" and note in life around me. I am reflecting only what I have been seeing. I also write professionally for journals. So if you think I am taking everything personally, it would be way off course. Then, I love pulling legs and twisting things to make the cat jump up a bit.

If you try to visualize me from my words, you may end up doing a lot of wondering.

My Mum calls me a joker and has wondered all her life when I would get down to live seriously. Now she has given up but she still feels I have the potential.....

You are right in saying you don't see me as that kind of person. I am not that worldly wise.

Janelle Portelli:

Hell yes, listening has only so made me too vulnerable and naked to the world who in return....have me grasping at the skill to be selfish to have a breath in me left, hell yes its too much, way so for one soul....I'm learning to be selective now as I'm just pulled into drama and fights over my alignment of concurrence.....hmmmm yes I feel better now....hail the other side....wise it can be and must so be to find a friggin balance in this crazy world....lol xxoo

Paul Schmolke:

Listening is easy, understanding what you hear is not so easy." I listened to what he said but heard what I wanted". Listening is half the battle, understanding is the other half. Many people can't really express themselves effectively as they lack skills with the language, so you listen to them and not understand what they are trying to communicate. Many others don't express themselves effectively because they don't understand what they are thinking. You may listen to either and not understand what they are trying to communicate because they lack the skill of understanding themselves or the words to express their ideas.

In the mind of the listener, what you have heard will be converted into what you are able to understand or what you are able to accept - either instance may be in error due to a poor command of the language or an inability to listen and hear without being judgmental.

Many speakers seek to veil their true meaning with clever speech; they are called politicians or attorneys. Criminals and con artists may do the same thing.

Most people will tell you the truth if you ask and many will reveal themselves in your first encounter with them if you just listen.

To listen effectively, turn off that part of your mind that wants to respond instantly and just listen. When the speaker is finished, digest what was said and respond to it then.

Janelle Portelli:

So very well articulated Paul....understanding and listening yes exactly....i get so pissed off (YES I DO I GET PISSED OFF!!!) when someone listens to about five words and are up to scratch on my whole point or story....and they are so sure they are running with it, I have not got anything out and I wonder who has butted in so quick and who the hell they are talking about or to whom, they have no idea what the hell I was going to say I wish I had $1 for every time I was actually misinterpreted as saying the exact opposite of what is interpreted before I finish one damn sentence.....yes, listen think then respond.....it's nice when it happens isn't it!!!! That's why I try to be selective and realise that if one has not heard then engaging is only going to be a struggle that can (YES I AM VULNERABLE AT TIMES) make me doubt myself at worst, although I see the ridiculousness in it all. I end up feeling misunderstood (which yes has happened) but I wonder if I'm nuts and speak backwards or am really speaking not with the mindfulness I so cultivate so communications are... yes... thought, articulated and not all mixed up.....

I still have moments of responding without listening properly...though I am usually very happy just goofing with friends or over excited on a new subject.....and laugh that I have probably missed most of what everyone was on about....least I don't state to know what the hell has gone on when I do it I guess...well most the time anyway.

I appreciate your answer Paul. Pradeep posts very insightful and reflective posts and I really appreciate those who spend time answering them as I find I really get a lot out of this.....yesterday I was one of those days I didn't feel like listening or understanding everyone else.

There is an exercise I do sometimes where I practice bare attention with people...it is amazing what comes out and how they feel drawn to you...it very simple though I can't remember the author that explains it just perfect...I am making a stab and guessing it could have been written by Mark Epstien Phd in his book 'Thoughts without a thinker', actually I think

I may be correct...it's a Buddhist mindset, he a western psychotherapist! I don't think you boys really need to read it though it is a good read although I was bit younger when I did.....not a usual book 23 year olds read as they think self development is fun and interesting, and other cultures and belief systems can be incorporated into our western society as they have great wisdom that can help you in life! xxoo take care friends......peace always j xxoo

Megha Pushpendra:

What a relief...i drank it all up...am a happy woman today.

Topic No 11

Megha Pushpendra **sir, would love to have your views on time management.**

PK:

There you have pressed the right buttons. Here I go. The first thing that comes to mind is this: Can time be managed?

When you say time management, I would think that you would like to control it like you do a river by either damming it or dredging or cleaning or whatever that we can do to it to make it work for you. It never occurred to me that this could be done with time. I thought about this for some time and I still don't get it.

Perhaps what you wish to say is "How can you manage yourself?" considering the time at your disposal. This would seem the more logical approach and the only one I can think of. Now if this is what you mean, then I wondered why ask me; not that I am averse to the idea. It is flattering to know that somebody cares about my thoughts enough to ask me. Millions of words by so called experts are being written and floating around and you still feel I may have something to say that would matter? How refreshing!

So let's discuss this in all seriousness. Time cannot be managed. All those who complain that they do not have time know fully well that they are showing off their self-importance. This is one way of showing that they have more of this world in their grasp in comparison to all the others who form a very large group on this planet who have nothing to do and are either looking for work and opportunity or are not "clever/able/qualified" enough to merit any attention in this world of ours where "IT" shows if you have it.

Then there are the hapless people who are a little woolly up there. They wake up with lovely intentions but then even a small butterfly can make them forget everything else and can make them first run for their camera and secondly after the butterfly. A few flowers on the way simply dash the entire timetable of the day to the ground and that is that. Now it is left open to your imagination if a butterfly can do this what would let us say would happen if a child needs this person or even an adult came around needing solace?

It would not be difficult to infer from the above that it is all in the mind. It is all relative to what we consider important and would like to spend the available time on. Then there is also the question of habits. We are more creatures of habits than we really wish to acknowledge. We act on impulses that have been inculcated into us by our surroundings and education. We give importance to these impulses and make them our flight-plan. They then decide the ETA. You are a virtual prisoner. If you are unhappy with the way things are working out in your day to day execution of time, then you need to look into all those tiny mental blips that point your way and chart your action plan. If you are not ready to look into that direction, then just forget it. Enjoy your 24 hours and get up next morning for another day of the same. A small example here would make my words clearer.

You are reading a book. You are engrossed in it. It is so interesting that it has you transfixed. Once in while you do remember to look at the clock.

The hubby will come home, the children will want dinner. Ok. Ok. You are aware of all this. But few pages more – let' say let's finish this paragraph... well I could safely stretch it to the end of the chapter and so on so forth till you have royally messed up your time-table. So that is that and there is no way to recover lost ground. All you can do is forget it and go on with your life. Just order a pizza and have a party. The kids will love it. The hubby will just be happy to have a bite of something-anything, instead of trying to keep awake with coffee. The book has more management control, over you than you on it. You were party to it. Where is the problem?

So what do you say? Shall we forget this utterly pointless subject?

Paul Schmolke

Do you have obligations to others? Do you understand how they view the obligations that you have made? If the answers are yes and they take the obligations seriously, then managing your time may be very important to their well being and yours. A mindful approach to living is all that is required. In other words, pay attention to your commitments. If you can't manage to do that then you have some work to do to improve your attitude about your obligations to others and yourself.

By the same token, if you have obligations to yourself and they need to be carried out in a timely way, you need to be mindful of how you handle them. An example might be taking medication for a heart condition or remembering to see a doctor.

One more example might be a shared obligation where your timely appearance is critical to someone else' needs. You need to consider their need and your schedule - like picking up your child from school so you can meet your wife for dinner out. Or making a court date so that your testimony can help to free an unfairly accused person and you will not be found guilty of contempt.

Each of these seemingly minor situations can become troublesome if a mindful approach to managing your time isn't given proper recognition. Many people are so self absorbed that they don't treat their obligations with respect. Over time, this can cause the loss of friends, business, and confidence in your dependability.

Mindful use of your time will probably help others make better use of their time and they will appreciate your efforts.

We have no control over the passage of time and we are unable to predict the future with any certainty so it could be argued that any attempt at time management is a waste of time. If you believe this, try it on your friends and business associates. I think that ample proof of the value of time and time management will become apparent to you very quickly.

The key is mindfulness, thoughtfulness, compassion and caring for others that may be affected by your actions.

Pradeep Pk Maheshwari :   Perfect note Paul

Paul Schmolke

Thanks for your kind comment. As a retired independent business person, I always took pride in being on time and delivering my work on time. I was a real estate appraiser, and everyone I dealt with would get very upset if deadlines were missed - either showing up late for an inspection or sending the report to the bank late was a big problem. I have always been pretty conscientious about managing my time but many others aren't. I have been in similar circumstances with most work I have done. It is really tough when the work requires artistic creativity and there is also a deadline to meet; As in Photography or Illustration work. But being mindful of the time always helped me.

Teya

Hello, dear Pradeep! This is the theme of my thinking lately.

I think that time management can only be a management of "your" activities. That You have clear goals in Your life and that You are making them come true. That You are aware of situations, connected to Yourself and that You pay attention to other, too. It can be difficult, but the effort is repaid. You can only find answers to your questions in yourself, although debating with others can help you sometimes, of course (and you are very thankful for this help).

Freedom, Love, Creativity - this is very important to me. To be active = to learn = to live. I love this!

Reality check gives you the opportunities to change something if you want. And as it is said: where there is a will, there's the way.

I wish You that 24 hours every day would be WONDERFUL for You, You are called to create them so. It's your opportunity and your decision, even blessing, make it count. Every step counts.

Globbler:

Pradeep, time management is a fascinating subject. It's life management through our thinking. Thank you for introducing this topic. I believe the best investment of our time is in self-discovery and self-improvement. As a voracious reader who has the passion to cover ground in all cultures and their literary heritage, I'm constantly searching for the most efficient way to do so. Any suggestions?

Pradeep Pk Maheshwari :

Oh yes. Make all your actions conscious ones with full concentration and focus and then you will see how much time is left to spare

Globbler:

Great point and great advice, Pradeep! Thank you and many blessings to you, my friend!

Topic No 12

Suicides and shooting sprees

From PK:

I have been rather concerned but now more than just worried about the regular news of students committing suicides because they are afraid of not doing well or failing in their exams.

Most attribute it to peer pressure and social pressures. But I feel there is something here that goes a lot deeper. I wish to study this subject a little more in depth.

There is also the subject of young people in schools going berserk and shooting etc.

I request you to give me your point of view and if possible, put me in touch with students and others so that I can get first hand understanding from the students themselves or their parents/friends teachers etc etc.

Dear Mr. Maheshwari,

The way student suicides are rising is indeed alarming. We have a whole bunch of kids who do not know what lies ahead and after hitting a road block for whatever reasons they simply end their life.

Most of the time it is their academics, or their relationship with the opposite sex, or their parents not being able to understand them as far as academics are concerned, or their learning being somewhat different from others... anything, in fact.

The problem, the way I see it, also lies in parents not being well-equipped to handle such situations. It can lead to not understanding what their child wants to do or desires to do.

Saurav Das

From"Aparajita Priyadarshini"

Yes Mr. Pradeep, you are indeed very right as this is not just about Peer Pressure. A major contribution towards this is from the School/College management and family as well. Well of course my views and opinions draw round my own experience.

When I was in 12th Standard one of my very close friend did commit suicide which resulted into major turn of events in our friend circle. 1 day prior to the event we all are very joyously playing cricket and the next day he committed suicide. It was his letter that helped us understand his decision.

It wasn't an impulse decision, he had been planning for months, he gave subtle hints to his parents as well about his problems in school but as he was an introvert he couldn't say much. He was fed up with the discrimination that a sportsman has to face in school. Those teachers' taunt still boils my blood, "You think you are Maradonna or what ???"

Well Yes he was indeed a Maradonna in making, if only people could understand his passion for sports & not for studies. He wanted to pursue his career in the same but never had the courage to say that to anyone else but his friends, as in India playing sports can be ones HOBBY but not CAREER. Unless of course its cricket. He wasn't able to handle the pressure from family to perform well in studies and also had faced enough hard times from the teachers. So he decided to QUIT.

We all raised hell in school and demanded for suspension of those teachers, which did happen eventually but what's the result. Today after 10 years when I go see my school there is no grass on the football field and the huge craters on basketball court make my heart ache. Those teachers were never suspended but transferred to another Govt School were now they are serving as Principals.

I was lucky to have a Dad (An Engineer) who encouraged me to take my own choice of career (Commerce) and stood by me in those dreadful school n college times (whn Non Science Students are treated as Non Achievers) but how many parents will keep their egos aside and do the same. Engineer ki Beti Engineer, Doctor ka Beta Doctor…. It's a normal scenario.

Regards,

Aparajita P

In answer to Aparajita's mail I had this to say:

This is very nice. It re-enforces my own view that at the base we are a nasty & narrow-minded people. More interested in imposing ourserlves than anything else. We do not spare our children, women or animals. We control ourselves only when we are afraid & know that the other party can do us harm or in sheer selfishness.

"Susan Connors"

Here's my simple (and quick for lack of time) point of view:

Children are no longer disciplined, thus they do not feel genuinely loved.

Today's children know that they can lie about their parents to a social worker and the social worker will most-likely believe them and not the adults. So, if a child decides to act out against a parent in order to get the love/attention they seek, the 'system' does not investigate and support the child getting what he/she needs -- just the opposite. What they get is further distancing and alienation from their parents. Children do NOT really want to be in control. They don't know how and when they turn to their peers, all they get is more confusion from other confused kids.

Whose fault is it? The adults in society who have abdicated their parental roles and tossed their kids to 'society' to raise. Society can't.

Susan

161

Phalgun Desai

"Today's competitive world where everything is judged by academic, monetary success makes students and young people see themselves as failures and not fit to live. Also single or unit families are the norm nowadays so support system at home is at times lacking...previously in joint-families, the support system was great."

"Ashutosh Labroo"

Dear Pradeep, You have raised a very sensitive & yet an extremely emotional subject for I think most of the INDIAN modern thinkers & parents. At least it is a very emotional subject for me as a parent. Hope my other friends will bear with me through a longish but important thought on the subject. The subject is really vast & I think if we go towards a dissection of this epidemic of giving up life in the wake of small term failures (that too if you call it so) the subject is too vast to be just debated. We need a revolution & a revolution is a VISION & nothing less.

We need the Govt, The Academicians, The Teachers, The Institutes & The Parents, The Society - all to come together & form an eco system which will change the very fabric of what cripples our children from enjoying "FAILURES". Yes, I really wonder why no one wants to teach how to FAIL. Everyone wants to teach how important SUCCESS is. Is that life is all about. It is today an equally important aspect we need to put emphasis upon.

I think deep down inside it is the spirit of competing put in a child since our childhood by the PARENTS, the SCHOOLS/ COLLEGES, the FAMILY overall & the SOCIETY at large. It is the education system & the social fabric of our country which puts a label on us by dividing people on grounds of ACADEMIC TALENT. To be honest, I am who I am with not much to remember which happened in my 24 Years of academic life. Really. I think it was the experiences of being & the learning around which shaped me & not the courses or schools or colleges.

I am willing to believe for people who love education as much as life, education is the experience but for me it was the experience around which made me a person I could.....

Moving on, so much is said about making it to IITs, IIMs & BITs or NITs. 90% is not any longer good enough to get admission anywhere. Why??? I don't think any entrance exams of any big institutes really even touches the nerve of who I am really? It gets to evaluate what society & the institutes want me to look like. How fake? I have a concern about the way TALENT is looked at in our country. Something we can certainly learn from the west especially.

So much so in spite of seeing how limited we are in sports or international arena of anything non-academic (except business). I wish for an INDIA where people, schools & parents are not inspired to raise a spirit less dry topper (No.1) who has to be the number 1 & nothing less, a doctor & nothing less, an engineer & nothing less, an MBA & nothing less. Comparisons galore if you fall!!! What for?

Well, if we think in the modern INDIA this epidemic has died, how wrong we are & do we still need evidence that something needs to be done to the EDUCATION FRAMEWORK of our SOCIETY & ACADEMIA. Hell yeah!!!

Yes, I am emotional as a modern progressive INDIAN like many of us to see how we haven't still given up on our conditionings as a parent & as a society at large. Just yesterday I went to a school to get my own daughter admitted & I saw hundreds of parents willing to go to any extreme to get their child admitted. Some were scolding their children to ensure they repeat what they are being told to mug up. How fake can we really get to be? Does that really help? Really, we need to introspect deeply today. At least my learning was to un-learn what I learnt from society about being a parent. Really, I think it was high time!!!

In the end, I wish to spare some thought on the teachers in institutes. I remember one of my teachers in school who used to throw a duster on a student who used to tell the wrong answers & then publicly humiliate people who would be in a tight spot. I still remember the loss of a very bright friend who committed suicide & actually was an excellent cricketer who went through this shock therapy.

I do wish many schools encourage & give equal footage to sports & extracurricular activities like music & social activities. Why can't we raise more TENDULKAR'S & SONU NIGAM'S & SANIA MIRZA's in our country?

If only our teachers would hold the hand of a weeping heart who just got the grades that he/ she so much dreaded (perhaps not so much due to himself as much for his parents/ peers & competitors) after the results & tell him "hey no worries, you will come around, see you are good in A, B & C, I will personally see to it that you do well in this too & yes this is not the end of the world & if your parents have a concern, I will speak to them?" Today it is about going that extra mile.

I think what I would like to see now is people going beyond the 90% syndrome. And one request I have for all believers in the 90% syndrome is to look at the biggest & the strongest achievers around them & let us look at what they learnt & what they scored. I think we will get an answer we need to understand & not ignore anymore. It is difficult & yet it is indeed the moment of truth. It is the ability to FAIL which enables a person for

SUCCESS forever. SUCCESS cannot be the destination alone if we don't love FAILURES equally. Quite deep!!!

Amen!!!!

With Love & Best Wishes,

ASHUTOSH LABROO,

Nirmal kumar wrote:

Subject: to teach how to FAIL - how to overcome failure.

To: "Ashutosh Labroo"

Hi , Sir I as a starter in this secret of life , dunno how to take the below mentioned statement , can we be taught how to overcome failure or how to face critical and sensitive issues; please correct me if I am wrong

Second thing I would like to know, how to overcome emotional situations, how to divert our mindset. Can anyone guide people or quote something to overcome this.

 I really wonder why no one wants to teach how to FAIL. Everyone wants to teach how important SUCCESS is. Is that life is all about. It is today an equally important aspect we need to put emphasis upon.

Regards

Nirmal

Dear Nirmal,

Thanks you for raising your query. I think especially in the life that we lead today we are running towards a goal so much so that we stop enjoying the pursuit of reaching their in its fullness.

I look at all failures as a milestone & at least my learning has been the more you fail, the more you learn how to succeed.

I loved what EDISON, EINSTEIN, LINCOLN, AMITABH, MICHAEL JORDAN, SACHIN TENDULKAR, JACK WELCH all taught the world around about failures. If you look at their lives, they all failed & sometimes they failed terribly & so much that some of us would have perhaps given up on dreams but they were in love with their pursuit & journey & I think they knew how to enjoy their failures.

When you enjoy your failures, you know how to overcome them. It is what you are afraid of the most & resist the most which you never get comfortable with. If you are not afraid or least bothered to fail you are more prepared to succeed.

See it like this, it becomes not so important as to "how to overcome failure" when you are "prepared to fail along the way". Right!!

Think about it & I am sure you will get to understand what I meant.

CHEERS!!!!

Ashutosh.

"Karthi Karthikeyan"

Dear Pradeep,

This is Karthik. Very glad to connect up with you as we share a common purpose. I speak to students in large groups and I drive this attitude of Self-Imaging and gratitude through real life experiences of people and examples. You are right; there is something that goes a lot deeper and the culprit is the belief and thoughts. What happens, "I play the game coolly; and yet I take results very seriously; instead play the game with passion and take the results coolly". Who said that a fail mark is total failure and a state first is a eternal success. A Survey was taken on the "Roll of Honour" of 50 schools of SSLC and HSc top scorers and it was found that 70% of them haven't been a "Roll of Honour" as on date. Now, it doesn't mean that they are failures. 20% of students who failed in 10th std 3 times and gave up studies are roaring in their fields and they continued their studies.

The joy of life is "Uncertainty"- we should have the wisdom of not connecting to these English words "Success" and "Failure", as at a point of time life teaches us a lesson and both doesn't hold any meaning. It is the meaning what "I" give.

169

The only purpose of life is:　Run till the finish line "come what may". In life, I can't change "Peer", "Parents" to talk and perform the way I want. But, I can respond to their stimuli, the way "I" want.

It would be an interesting dedication to the youth which is 50% of Indian population (18 years to 28 years, bear with me if there is error in this range...10-20%), who indeed would be shaping the tomorrow of our nation.

regards,

Karthik

From: jesna sivasankar

Hi friends

As I was reading through the mails I was wondering whether there is anything called a failure...and I don't understand why we give too much emphasis on that word. The word Failure itself gives a negative vibration to every individual. This in fact stops human beings to take up any positive energy he has, to succeed; even though we keep on saying Failure is the stepping stone to success. If failures are stepping stones to success there should be more success than failures as people 'by make' has a tendency to move towards success than wasting life, energy and time over failures. If we are not able to do that...then there is something wrong.

Why don't we just change that to Feedbacks????

Failure, I feel should be taken as Feedbacks and feedbacks are always positives, are giving space for learning and has the immense quality to upgrade oneself. As human beings we associate ourselves positively or negatively with words as they are outcome of our experiences and this has created a problem when it comes to words associated negatively to our mind. May be this is one reason why people can't take up failures positively and this lesson should start of with the primary institution - The FAMILY. Once this happens there will be more success be it the 90% craze or what ever... our insight would become more polished and the more polished it becomes the more we enjoy a life of fulfilment.

There is no point in asking anyone else to change their thinking pattern in this way unless we start to practice it. I am doing it ... friends let us begin it in our own life... and we will spread it across.... what do you say????

Katherine Siswick-Clark:

171

I think that the teenage years are an important time for a soul. Teenagers are no longer children but they are not thought old enough to do everything things for themselves and they are still answerable to their parents/careers. It is a time of self discovery and I think that there many pressures on young people to be a certain way with their friends, family as members of society...there are many expectations on them and many judgments too, all of this makes it challenging for young people to really know themselves and be themselves. Teenagers need to be able to express themselves and they need to feel safe and accepted to do that and it is here that I feel is where the change needs to occur. Confidence and self esteem are huge issue for young people. Feeling safe, accepted and loved so crucial along with having a deep connection with their inner self and their joy ⍰

Pradeep Pk Maheshwari Yes. This is the problem essentially. You talk of the problem in teenagers. I am seeing it already in my 5 year old. We adults need to change ourselves and our attitudes towards children as hapless products - extensions of ourselves and us as their owners.

Katherine Siswick-Clark:

"Yes Pradeep I do think it is something that is evident at all ages and you are right that too many parents think that their children are "their's" and not individual souls with their own destiny and purpose. I think our primary role as a parent is to be an example, if we can discover and be ourselves and develop positive and healthy coping mechanisms then our children will learn from us to do the same.

172

Edward Stanulevich IV commented:

"Here in American, we are disconnected as a community. There is little social support for people. There is no respect for others. In some subcultures suicide is romanticized. Think Romeo and Juliet, and the emoting stuff (I do not get the emoting thing at all).

I think kids lose their perspective about their place in the world and over indulge in self pity. They think their problems are much worse than they are. We have a fast food, want it now mentality here too. We do not think we need to work for things. We do not appreciate how good we really have it. These factors can be overwhelming to deal with alone. So, thinking that they cannot bear the pain of life, the end it.

Also, the sensationalist news media is quick to pick up these kinds of negative stories. Bad news sells. It can also have an influence on how a culture looks at its self. As suicides become publicized more, they become more common. This could lead to more suicides.

I blame the TV for not taking better care of the kids. It could not possibly have anything to do with how parents no longer raise their kids in our culture.

Not that I am blaming any one individually, it is a cultural factor, so even parents who are involved in their kid's lives may not be able to do enough to overcome the power of culture.

We have also become accustomed to children having a higher survival rate than they did 100 years ago. So the death of a child has a bigger impact on us as it occurs at a lower percentage rate than it did back then.

Steve Lochmueller *Makes a point that I think is awfully pertinent and we in India did not allow this to happen too much but the trend for imports is catching up.*

"I certainly agree with your assessment. I would add however, that some of these suicides are indeed caused by societal pressures. The new global economy has shifted manufacturing jobs to other nations causing a shift to service/supply type jobs that for years were filled with younger people working their way into the job market. These positions are now being filled with displaced workers from other fields causing increased competition for employment. This dynamic coupled with the move by many employers to require higher education for virtually any position has increased the pressure for our younger people to succeed in school or face the possibility of not being suitable for employment. The realization of this in a capitalistic society becomes overwhelming for some simply because we are creating a nation of two classes, the rich and the poor. Those unable to "properly" market themselves are relegated to a life of servitude without proper compensation."

Pradeep Pk Maheshwari -My comment on the above:

I saw the devastation of the economy and job market in France since 30 years ago where I was once thinking of establishing base. I understood this factor early and ran back to the protected atmosphere of India.

They give no earning power to the masses but want them to buy all the goodies which they promote with religious fervour.

Dave Shapiro:

"As a suggestion....While educating the parents is most important, the level of dysfunction in many of these homes prevents honest communication, a real understanding of what each family is experiencing and bottom line...honesty"

Having worked in many school districts and working with counsellors, students, psychologists and parents...most of the motivators are already identified. Most are now even aware of the triggers for these behaviors but there the progress stops. The motivations for each disaster seem somewhat related...i.e. poor self image, depression, harassing, poor parenting, bullying, and peer pressure and on and on....

Globbler commented:

175

"Pradeep, your concern reveals your good heart, my friend, and I am grateful to be your friend. This tragedy is a result from the lack of inspiration, motivation, and education. Many young people become victims to the negativity that is presented daily through all media channels. How different would our world be if news, movies, radios, Internet were predominantly focused on inspirational, motivation, and educational positivism? The message of understanding, love, and peace has been marginalized. Yet a group like ours is a beacon of hope and positive energy in the Universe. As Gandhi said, "A small body of determined spirits fired by an unquenchable faith in their mission can alter the course of history."

THE ILLUSION OF VIRTUE.

Of all the tricks of illusion we get to see, this is the biggest that humanity has played on itself. What an absolute control it has on everybody's sight and mind. Even if somebody helps us see through the whole game, the chances are that we would still like to keep our eyes closed and live with the illusion. How do I begin to explain myself? Since the beginning of time males and the females of the species have been playing with each other. What harm could there be in it? Yet somewhere along the way certain values were established and the play came under the rules and regulations of elders who promptly called it a sin. This gave them the right to censure and control the lives of their brethren. The brethren for some reason found it perfectly alright as the men specially could call the shots and control the lives of their women and possessions, and women acquiesced because it suited them too in some pervert way.

This was not the only rule that took the form of sin or/and virtue but definitely the most mind arresting. These rules of what are sins and what is not virtuous rules our lives to such an extent that we have forgotten to live our lives. The only concept that matters is to be seen to be virtuous. A little introspection will show us that most of our actions are based on our need to be seen as virtuous. A deeper look around will show us how in the name of doing good for the good of others we meddle in the lives of others and give birth to hurt and mishaps. It even absolves us from looking at ourselves and improving ourselves which is "the" tragedy of human existence to my way of thinking. Once we are in this mode we can so conveniently keep on pointing fingers at others and in comparison seem so wondrously divine.

Let us begin with the legal aspect of illegal activities. Things and activities which are personal and were giving no trouble to anyone suddenly became illegal and gave the police a baton to wave around. This power has often seen to have gone to their heads and they misuse it for their own pleasure or show of virtue. Have you noticed with what glee they announce that they have broken a prostitution ring? Come to think of it, how much detective prowess is needed to find an entry into a madam's "kotha"(house of pleasure)? This class of work which was once an indispensable part of the cultured life which gave rise to such eminent dancers and singers like Umrao Jaan (famous courtesan of 18th century)) is today bearing the brunt of the moral police and often creating situations where the constabulary is able to get away with rape.

There are of course other institutions that have legalized this profession because it suits the rulers. We are all aware of the institution of temple "dassi" where the damsel is married to the Lord and dances for him and is bedded by His servants. Then take the very common institution of marriage in which more women are battered than they are cherished. If it is legal it is fine. Even fathers get away with rape of their daughters because it is happening within the confines of the marriage and the laws permit no interference here in the name of virtue and sanctity of marriage. The whole society looks on and calls it a personal matter.

Had it not been for the laws, we would not have so much of the police force wasting their time in stopping such innocuous activities and also wasting scarce resources of both the judiciary and the detective force. But I suppose it suits everybody. A huge trade is based on this illegality with huge sums involved. Trading in women, enslavement and stealing of children are just some of the activities that I can mention; add to this side dishes like illegal distilling and use of alcoholic drinks, pornography and paedophile activities and you will see what a witch's brew we have here.

I wonder if the law makers ever give thought to the disaster they are giving rise to when they make a law. Take for instance the crack down on marijuana. This has been the staple diet of the common man for centuries and no rule ever condemned it. But the new-age governments have ruled it as obnoxious and made it illegal; one would think they would relent when it has been conclusively proven that it helps seriously sick patients in controlling their pain. But no, they are too virtuous to let such nefarious products to contaminate our lives! Other strong opiates are so stringently controlled that the sums involved in successfully trafficking them go into astronomical figures. The temptation to trade in it is too great for the frail spirit of human-kind to resist. There is a concerted effort by the traffickers to hook people and create clients for them. If only the law makers would get off their virtuous backsides and understand that this is not the way to go about it. It is their stupid laws and little understanding of applied psychology that is making this planet a vice-den. Yet cigarette smoking is ok even with all the data saying it is really the most hurtful of human activities today.

India has one of the most stringent laws in the world regarding what women can do to fight for their rights. The anti-dowry and harassment laws are draconian to say the least. Beware of your wife. If she gets into the mood to play a fast one on you, all she has to do is to call the police and after that the legal machinery takes over. They arrest you and your immediate family and put you behind bars first for a week at least and then only ask questions. Investigations are more from the point of view to nail the man rather than find out if there is any basis of truth in the allegations. The whole process works on the basis that if the weaker sex is complaining there has to be some truth in it. After all only the male of the species is known to be malicious. Women on the other hand are made of sugar and spice and all things nice. It is another matter that it is now common knowledge that more often than not whenever a woman is upset and looking for her demands to be met, she is using the police and judiciary to harass and threaten the man into submission if she can.

The list of such misplaced and misunderstood actions is long and can be seen in every phase of life. That parents are "loving" and cherish their children is one myth. That beggars are forced into begging because they are without other options is another. When we go to temples to bribe the Lord into granting our wishes and then save our souls by giving alms to the beggars outside, do we ever stop and wonder that it is an organized syndicate at work? There are of course exceptions so let's not get into an argument. It is also true that our virtuous conduct has given rise to a profession and a very unscrupulous group of people who indulge in stealing children, maiming them, and turning them into professional beggars and then live on their proceeds. Don't think that beggars don't pay taxes and are free to roam. They have territories and whatever administrative authority is in control of that territory, takes their cut from them. Many beggars are rich beyond their needs; miserliness having become a habit. So much for our virtuous conduct! If you are a believer in Karma, then think again; what are you really reaping?!!

50 years ago, the only touch with the outside world an individual had in India and many other countries for that matter, was through the cinema. This was not only a land where fantasies were played out, but where people met and asked each other out. It was the central focus of our society. Young impressionable minds were certainly affected. This was in those times when society was more conservative than it is today and I can say, more tolerant too. Otherwise will somebody explain to me why no voices were raised when the boys teased the girls and why the suggestive cabaret dances in drinking bars were never blocked from being screened? What was the law saying then and where was the censor board? Even when the teasing scenes became more violent, nobody raised their voices. This was what two whole generations of youth saw and of course, found it acceptable. And now that we have entered the 21st century, suddenly the Indians have found religion in its worst form and intolerance too. With religion have come the moral brigades and the violence of

people who refuse to let others live their own lives. The truth is that we have ourselves to blame with our virtuous, saintly non-interfering outlook. Now it is too late. The script has been lost and it will have to be written all over again. The tragedy is that the TV and the pulp media are adding to the fire. Nothing is left to the imagination. It is even getting to be boring. But the fact remains that the average human is in a state of constant titillation. The young ladies in real life with their dresses or the lack of it are making it worse. It seems that they have a right to titillate but the young men are expected to maintain a saintly self-discipline. I maintain that our elders have failed us; they have failed in showing the way and instilling in their young the discrimination needed to wander in this wide wicked world.

In many countries, in the last century, virtue reared its head in the form of "Prohibition" to stop both manufacture and consumption of alcohol. Every time it only increased the illegal activity in its manufacture and consumption and unscrupulous elements made hay while it lasted. Yet every time a vote-catching line is needed, prohibition is the answer and is practiced every now then by our state governments. We never seem to learn. The voters fall for it every time and the leaders are always willing because it not only brings them to power but becomes a source of income as they prove to be the biggest behind-the-scene law-breakers.

Ever notice how often everything in life is done only for your good? You would have heard this explanation from parents, elders, kin, teachers and associates at work. Never does anyone ever say that they are doing it because they want to and that there is more often than not their own gratification or profit in it. From the sound of it, we are all living very saintly lives, with no ulterior motives at all.

Ana Prpic:

I like your post and agree with your observations. Why do people behave this way, and I know I'm sometimes like that too, I really don't know, but would like to. All the psychology books I have read so far haven't made it much more clear, or better said, they did help me understand, but where to find answers how to make things better I don't know. I don't like this world my children grow in, but maybe it's just nostalgia and sign of getting older?

Pradeep Pk Maheshwari:

Dear Ana, from the occult point of view, we here believe that the human is not yet a cohesive whole - what we call properly individualised. The so called human person is basically made of three main components - the material, the emotional and the mental beings. These three have got together to create a human person of today but are not as yet in full harmony with each other. All the three have distinct personas and have very separate realms of existence. These realms are all pervading yet self contained. That is why you see such contradictions in individuals and split personalities are a recorded fact.

This is why you see people behaving in certain ways and never learning from their experiences or any change ever coming into them. After a certain time of let's say 24 years at the most, people just grow old perpetuating their personas and eventually die out.

Ana Prpic: Well, this is interesting; could you tell me where you got this info from?

Pradeep Pk Maheshwari: You should read Sri Aurobindo and the Mother of Pondicherry.

Pradeep Pk Maheshwari

Dear Ana, here is a simplified explanation.

The body - the physical/material envelop works at Mother Nature's speed. It operates on an instinctive guidance system that operates without any conscious knowledge. As the persona evolved, to that slowly got added the emotional being and the mental being.

At the present state of things, the emotional being takes pleasure from the activities available to it through the body. It is only interested in its own enjoyment - what we see as selfishness, cleverness, gossip, boasting, cheating, jealousy, anger, lusting etc.

The mental being for the time being is attached to the body and emotional being and uses all its faculties of reasoning, analysis & logic to further the demands of the emotional being & body merger. All the three are bumbling along merrily. Very few people really ever get the opportunity to develop the mind fully. Very few even care.

What is not known or understood is that most of the emotional beings that Sri Aurobindo has named as Vital beings feed on the emotions of human beings. And their purpose is served only when the humans are agitated although it also serves to teach humans lessons from the tragic consequences. So they keep on initiating situations which result in mayhem. But these beings if taught to look further are also ready to change and then put all their energies into positive actions. Then you see altruism, kindness, compassion, forgiveness, tolerance etc in action.

The mind (The Mental Being) is still too young into this game but it is waking up and taking control slowly. Through the mind we can reach other worlds and beings. Now it depends on us, the maturity we show. The discipline we have been taught/learnt from experience and we are prepared to follow.

A whole lot depends on the programming the mind has received in the formative years. This programming ultimately governs the journey of one's life and as the programming is in the subconscious parts, very difficult and very averse to change. That is why habits play a bigger part in our lives than the mind in action.

Topic No.14

The Illusion of Honesty

The entire social management on this earth is based on the presumption that human being are upright and honest beings loaded up to the gill with positive attributes. Added to this is the blinkered view that the human animal is always looking forward, progressive, dying to excel, reasonable, committed, clear in his mind, basically sincere in word and action, with rarely any hidden agenda of his own and what not. Let's be a little sincere for once and look into the subject honestly; we are anything but. The above presumptions although taken as the base for everyday management, are prominent only in their absence. Anyone who proves himself to be really endowed with these qualities is soon dubbed and canonized a saint.

Why am I taking up this subject today? Because in the recent past I had the experience of seeing this paradox in action in two very clear cut incidences. Take the legal system for instance. The entire process of governing a country and making the laws is based on the understanding of the basic nature of humans one would suppose. Evidence in the courts is collected on the basis of an oath on the Bible, Koran or the Gita or some such basis. Does the keeping of one's hand on a lifeless book convert us into unshakably honest citizens? If this were true then why are paid witnesses to be found and the word perjury ever came into existence? So the legal system as practiced is flawed but we have to live with it. The question mark on the credibility of the accuser is also raised. That the defender would lie to save his skin does not require any intelligent double-take.

The other day I was with a lawyer friend who was listening to the client's version of things in a criminal case. The client was the accuser and kept on evading a proper answer to a particular question. It was becoming obvious the client was not being forthright in his answer but until he confided fully the lawyer had no way to coerce him into telling him the truth. I was watching and wondering when this game would end. It is so simple to understand that if the lawyer is required to do a good job, he needs to know the truth; but "no", the client was seeking to obfuscate matters and manipulate matters with little or no idea of the due process of law. It was difficult to explain to him that even if he was the accuser and the injured party there is such processes as cross-examinations, corroborative witnesses and circumstantial evidence. The client saw only his side of things and in his cleverness saw his word being accepted at absolute face-value as final. The lawyer was having a hard time. Poor guy had the choice of being honest and be brusque with the client with the possibility of losing him and his income or go along, do his job as best as he could under the circumstances and pocket his fees; letting the client to fend and pay for his attitude as destiny beckoned.

Well, when it is a matter of money making and exercising the little of control available to us in this life, we all tend to slip a bit. But it becomes extremely surprising to know that there are people who hurt their own selves too but cannot come clean. Take the relationship between doctor and patient. The life of the patient depends on the doctor. Nevertheless few people are totally honest with their doctor.

In a more general way let us peep into our lives too. I see that all of us are playing games. Busy with the nonessential and the process of creating an image all around of being virtuous, generous and full of other good qualities, yet at heart fully selfish and naughty, if not downright malicious. I do not deny that there is no dearth of basically honest people; but the fact remains that we do have a propensity to prejudices, tendency to jump to conclusions and be titillated by juicy gossip; and not always honest in our listening, seeing and re-reporting. If you want to see the human animal in action, just see a sales guy in action or read the advertisements and brochures put out by companies for their products.

The relationship between sexes is called the battle of the sexes; why so? Because at the core all he male wants is his cuddle and the female her security. But to get to his cuddle, see the male's fabrication of the pedestal to soften up the female; and the female not to be outdone, letting the male get away with it all. What a spider's net we create around us for trapping ourselves.

This reminds me of a story I came across again recently. A man, it seems, someone came to the great philosopher Socrates to relate to him a juicy piece of a story about someone. Socrates said that he would listen to the story only if it passed his triple filter test of it being first undeniably and absolutely surely true, second if it was something good in import and content and third if it was useful in any way. The man had to admit that it was neither of the three and Socrates refused to hear it.

I wonder if we applied this rule of Socrates in our lives how much of it would remain standing?

Ana Pyxis:

Socrates seems to have learnt from Buddha "If you propose to speak, always ask yourself, is it true, is it necessary, is it kind." Or, is it the other way around?

Doesn't matter, anyway, I think not a lot would remain.

Pradeep Pk Maheshwari:

Ana, these sayings in any group you go to, you will see, these have been attributed to every great thinker by their followers.

I think most of these sayings go back before all the names they are attached to. If you study the stories in the sacred books of all religions, you will find many common factors. All saying the same thing but a little differently adapted to the local conditions.

Did you know that the Ten Commandments can be found even in Hinduism. So is the story of The Deluge and the Ark; Crossing of the sea and regaining freedom etc

The Snake and the Bull are revered in our mythologies like they were in Crete and even before that?

The priests in South India wear the same hairstyle and dress as we see on tombstones found in Turkey of cultures 3000 yrs old or maybe more and those going for Haaj to Mecca? etc etc

I greatly admire the French saying: There is nothing new under the sun.

Ana:

So true. And if we don't search ourselves no one is going to serve it to us. I stumbled upon the Zeitgeist movie on the net and was quite amazed at some of the things they discuss in it. So many connections between religions, for example, so many same concepts in them, only said in a different way. Is it naive to wish, to believe that maybe one day others will see it too?

Pradeep Pk Maheshwari:

When we are working on ourselves (not just talking about it) and creating something lasting in the earth's consciousness, we are sowing seeds that will sprout one knows not where. So let's do our bit. Eventually, others will see it too but it may not be now.

Steve Lochmueller:

I have looked in the mirror, and 2 out of 3 ain't bad :)

Seriously though, I would enjoy a world that functioned by this rule. I believe the world would be far more substantial if it did. 98% of the world's wealth is controlled by 2% of its population and the world suffers because of it. People are actually considered to be and are referred to as human capital by those that rule. Society has created and perpetuated this ideal of honesty and virtue in order to maintain control over the masses. The average person doesn't desire to be dishonest, but how many "so-called wealthy" people bother themselves with this rule? Can you name an individual of "power" or "standing", a corporation or government that abides by this rule? To be sure there may be a few, but the vast majority uses our obedience to this rule against us to further acquire power and wealth.

I am not suggesting that we simply ignore virtue and honesty, but when we are required by our government to generate wealth or face punishment of imprisonment or repossession of homes for failure to pay tribute (taxes) to our rulers, then the rule we would rather follow must at times be set aside for the greater good of providing for families.

Imagine what the world would be had the ruling class never been allowed to manipulate us.

Imagine the standard of living for the world's population if greed and power struggles never existed.

The amount of wealth and resources spent on waging war throughout history for the purpose of obtaining more wealth and resources could have easily provided for a world without hunger, without wanting, or needing.

So having said all that, I suppose I must admit that you are correct in saying that Virtue and Honesty are nothing more than fanciful concepts of fairy tales and that humanity is mostly comprised of the dishonest and non-virtuous.

Dave Shapiro:

What about just saying animal nature sometimes over powers human nature?

Richard Schooping:

Leaves falls away and new leaves fill that space. Be mindful; for it is also through deep and focused analyzation that one becomes attached to the waves of change, and is also now playing a role. There is more than judgment to realize concerning our experience, as you know. And I do agree that one should not pretend. We are to fully own ourselves in each moment to "see" our experience clearly. Ultimately, a person needs to know themselves, and owning the steps they have taken brings insight and wisdom.

Side-tracking a bit:

Pradeep Pk Maheshwari **Are you sticking to your wife/husband/partner/friend because you like to or because for many reasons (legal/habit/social/convenience or other) you aren't able to do otherwise?**

Gro Viste:

It's not important what reason you have to keep staying where you are, as long as it is what is right for you and you are happy for it. Everybody has their own history and background so they choose how they choose.... The important thing for me is that I CAN choose..

Patricia Loya:

Left a husband of 23+ years, his alcoholism became intolerable, loved the old him very much, loved the old man he was and never thought I would leave him. Left with car, dog, clothes and computer and he sunk so far into depression, he lost his $100,000+ job and our home and two rentals all went to foreclosure. Could I have arranged/coordinated it better? Sure, but I did not have the ability and four years later I still say I did the best I could.

Pradeep Maheshwari:

Primarily the question was aimed at those who cannot afford to break up. Yet....Patricia, you have raised another question which is also very or more important. When we have decided to break up what is our feeling?

I suppose you wanted him to feel the hurt that you felt and you destroyed him as he had your life. He did have it coming to him. In your case are you sure it was not your unavailability in spirit and action that made him go towards alcohol as would a big sulking baby?

What I have seen is that in our present state we have given too much importance to "loyalty" and not enough to "caring". It has resulted in a lot of stress and wild behaviors. We should study the Polynesian cultures; Where partnering has been given a slightly more friendly importance. I think we involve our egos in our partnerships and complicate matters.

Another topic is sex. For instance, take the importance of sex. Sex has its place but it is not everything. Friendship is what makes the life go around.

In our present state of mental conditioning, we go overboard if there is any deviation by a partner in sexual partnering. Women need to understand that men have deep love for their wives and the relationship is important to them but they can still want a romp if available. Like a good cup of coffee.

But once this is given the cap of "cheating"(illegality/sin) - it becomes a serious hurt and the tendency then is to hurt back - and hurt hard.

The lies we live?!

Patricia Loya:

No - u are way off. I never wanted to hurt him. Never. Interesting that you would read it that way.

Pradeep Maheshwari: **Just raising a point. I understand that things come to such a pass that there is little left as an alternative. Even though we do not wish to, the step has to be taken. Many individuals choose a path/destiny which simply is not partnerable. Parting of ways becomes imperative.**

Janelle Portelli: Yes, but although so may be true... why does this make us right to loose our humanity or empathy for such souls who may fall, is this not a lesson we all learn maybe in varying degrees and consequence, do we still see????

The Club of Givers

When we give something we are always keeping a track of every penny that is going out but when we are receiving something we feel that we have never received enough. And then we compare our giving with what is coming in and always the final analysis shows a negative balance because compared to what we have given we have never received our due.

Are we being true to ourselves and the universe which is organizing our lives around us? There is so much expectation from the universe but to receive we have to be in the club of givers without premeditated calculations of why & what.

When we give our youth, time and energy to family, relationships, work we do so with an intent which is very self-oriented at the core. No conditionals!

The joining of the club of givers requires, spontaneity, the opposite of the tendency to hoard, live with less and as far as possible with the minimum one can. At the same time sharing of goods, effort and time because somebody is genuinely in more need than you and could obviously put whatever you are parting with to better use. Finally the belief that the Universe is there and will give what you need anyway.

The best givers are intensely alive and very involved in life. When you drop the critical, calculating and the judgmental attitude, there is an aura of compassion which builds up around you. Then you can only give. I know many millionaires in this group and I have been blessed by the help they gave me in cash, kind and personal time.

As an exercise, study your life and see how many things are lying around you that are never used and list them out. Second step if you feel there are others who can use them and NEED them, would you be ready to pass them on?

This is living in the present. Things come and go. We are only caretakers or users for a while; like a coin which changes hands hundreds and thousands of time in its life time. Yet the humans have been able to delude themselves into believing that things belong to them. These people close their doors so effectively that nothing goes out from them nor anything comes in to them. What a waste of a lifetime - it is so sad; these people are doomed to repeat their lifecycles over and over.

So how does one open out to the universe; How to be a witness? How do I grow out of the petty self? It is simple really. See the world with benevolent eyes. Don't judge - observe as a third party witness. And above all: don't try to change the world. Identify yourself with beautiful things and surround yourself with them.

Learn about all the things that are negative in character, like noise, obnoxious materials, obnoxious emotions etc - anything that leaves a bad after-taste, shocks or frightens or as the environmentalists would says polluting. Try to distance yourself from these. And then join the club of givers. You'll see things will start falling in place.

Simrin Haz: There is a saying for a woman who has a wardrobe of clothes, "Those which have not been touched by many a moons, please do give it away, for it is of no use to you". But how many of us actually do this, we seem to cling to things like slippers and shoes which just decorate our racks , torn T- shirts ,empty plastic containers and unused records and CD's. What makes us not want to be in The club of Givers?

Pradeep Pk Maheshwari:

The pettiness of our own minds/personas?

Or

The feeling that when things that have been identified with our personas, go out of our lives, something of us is breaking away too?

Topic No 16

Eyes Wide Shut

Normally, the newspaper arrives around 7 in the morning and I pick it up soon after. But one day I left early in the morning and the paper was not picked up. The paper boy had left it, as usual, near the front door in the passage leading from the main gate to the front door. So it was glaringly in the way. A big black and white spread on gray cement, dead in the middle of the open space with no clutter around it. The milkman came at eight, walked right on it to enter the house and went out the same way; totally missing the sight of the paper. When I returned at 9 or so, the mud stamped-by-footprints paper put my hackles up but that is another story.

The next day I asked the milkman why he had walked all over the paper instead of picking it up or at least he could have avoided stepping on it. His reply was simple that he did not see it! This got me wondering. Some years ago we had another milkman, who used to tell us about his car and the buses he was plying on Delhi's road. He was not driving himself but leasing the buses out. It seems he owned two. The other day the postman whose normal time to visit is after midday, arrived at 9 in the morning and I asked him what happened. What he was delivering was yesterday's post. He had missed delivering it yesterday because the driver of a bus that he plies on Delhi's roads did not come and he had to drive it himself.

This raises two questions. Who are behind the buses that are supposedly killing one or two people everyday on Delhi's roads? The newspapers inform us that many of the buses are in actuality owned by policemen and other political dignitaries so that when a complaint or misdemeanor is noticed, the concerned people look the other way. But I think that the malaise is deeper than that. The authorities are looking at the problem with eyes tightly shut. When they ordered the buses to be checked, they conveniently forgot to focus on the point that the buses by themselves are inert pieces of machinery. The fault has to be with the people responsible with their upkeep and more so the driving and people skills of the staff running them.

A bit of mayhem is to be expected if people from the community of milkmen and rough and tumble farmers are running the buses and their adored young ones are driving them; quite often without any training or self-discipline in their character. If my milkman can miss a two whole square feet of white spread with black markings in a small passage with nothing else around it, do you think that these people would be sensitive to the needs of being careful in any situation?

If we focus on the buses alone we shall miss the forest. The point is that most of us live lives immersed in a sea of denials. We do not see because it is not convenient to see.

We do not listen because it is not convenient to hear.

We speak without meaning a single word and if necessary we would deny having spoken. We are shutting off the world around us but want the world to remain open to us and not only that; we want the world to make the required effort to reorganize itself to suit our fancy. This is surely the perfect recipe for disasters.

The other day I spoke of people driving as if the other vehicles were there for decorative purposes only. Every driver thinks that he is the only one important and of course the honking of the horn would make it clear to anybody. They zigzag around other vehicles as if the others were stationary and miss hitting each other by hair's breadth. The bad habit of motorcyclists coming from behind and shooting themselves in front of your bumper, forcing you to brake to avoid hitting them is now an acceptable manoeuvre. Every single motorcyclist does it. They cram shelves in the minimum of spaces between vehicles and if they are brushed they come out to fight.

The surprise is that they are not crushed more often. I wonder if the buses are really to blame all the time. My thoughts always veer towards blaming the two wheelers when I read about another death. Why can't we keep a little distance between each other when driving to allow for errors and mistakes of judgment or even technical snags? Are we so used to living shoulder to shoulder that we practice it even with our vehicles? What is the point in blaming the vehicles? They are as good as the ruffians behind the wheels. What needs correction is our attitude of "Me; Cant-you-see Brilliant, Able & Smarter Guy, so Me come First"!

Babuji Bose:

Wisdom words ... how have other countries/cities been able to get better driving discipline, Delhi, Lagos, Bangkok traffic discipline remains low?

Pradeep Pk Maheshwari:

Sense of responsibility towards each other is the factor. Where it is lacking, chaos will be seen.

Simrin Haz:

Where do you reside Mr Maheshwari? Reading your tirade it seems you are a resident of the capitol Delhi, or some city in UP? Yes, nobody has any time for anybody! It is always ME as this topic implies!!

Pk Maheshwari:

Well, it seems as if I am focusing on traffic but this is so because it is visible to all and leaves not much space for argument. The focus is principally on our myopic characters. Can we live as if others do not exist?

Dave Shapiro:

For many, our vehicles are an extension of self....Here in the west, many kids put "BIG" tires on their trucks, in Europe many use small cars for economy and parking, in China and India, bicycles are the cheapest and easiest way to get around. In all cases, there are ass holes on the roads so watch your butt...

Johnny Lindquist:

I think that having full control over a deadly object such as a hunk of metal that goes far faster than any human on foot, should be a difficultly earned right and privilege. Here in America, children at the confusing age of 16 are able to take a far too simple test, then given the same auto rights as a fully competent adult...never expected to take a driving test again for the rest of their lives, despite eye-sight changes, later developed mood disorders, injuries, etc.

It seems to me that only certain, and a select few, amount of people are mechanically inept enough to operate and comprehend the logistics of such motor vehicles, and should be an earned privileged for those select few. Why must every person have the right to drive these potential 'death machines' around with such ignorance and foolishness?

People can carpool. Take mass transit. Work closer to home. In fact, lesser vehicles on the road would be far better for the Earths' health anyway.

Pradeep Pk Maheshwari:

You couldn't have said it better. The things we allow in the name of freedom and then curtail it in other matters which are really personal. When the car came into being about a century ago, an Indian sage called it "the devil incarnate". The human being on the average has little or no sense of balance and discrimination - specially at the early ages of 12-22 or so. Yet parents who are supposed to be intelligent/mature adults do not show any inclination to stop their children or change laws. And then the kids are allowed to drink alcohol to their fill, take their cars out and straight on into a wall/tree/railing or some such convenient barrier.

Why do we need armies? All we need to do is collect a million cars on the border of a country we wish to invade, give them free to kids - with a promise of a fortune if they reach the other side of the border, with another lucrative offer of a girl as co-passenger and unleash them on the offending country.

I find it very amusing to see people taking out their car to go out a few steps round the corner. As if when not surrounded by the sheath of their car, they are nothing. On one side, we talk of safety, less speed and "warming" and at the other end we keep churning out more cars, faster cars and give credit to buy them.

In India I see buy people living in crowded jungles, buying the biggest car with no parking space to call their own. I ask people - Do you realise that you are leaving your most expensive object that you own out on the street? Do you need it for travel or to show off?

I wonder where people get a chance to try out their sports coupes.

In India people are using their children to ferry them around; no license or proper training! The kids learn to hold the steering and that is considered enough. The police are too busy making money to stop them.

In contrast I remember my father, who never let me touch his car all thru his life - he never considered me a fully grown up person at all! I must say, my wife sees me in the same light but allows me to drive.

Johnny Lindquist:

Stupid facebook. I wrote an entire reply, and at the press of some mysterious button, it all wiped away.

Essentially, I had said well put on your part.

And it seems to come down to vanity. I think that maximum legal speed limit in this country is 80, but in most states it's 70. 60 or 55 in the cities. Sports cars can go twice the max. For what purpose? To show off? Avoid the police?

And the size of many vehicles these days is ridiculous. I always seem to see the tiniest of woman in the largest vehicles. And they are almost always driving alone.

We have a long way to go in this world before we can ever reach a point where we can all live together. And it's the "little" things like this, and so much else that should be our first steps.

Pradeep Pk Maheshwari:

And we are the "intelligent" beings that dream of populating the universe!

Johnny Lindquist:

As of now we have more characteristics of a virus. In regards to the damage we are doing to our planet.

Edward Stanulevich IV:

Don't worry. Nature will take care of everything.

Everything is impermanent.

This means you and me too!

Johnny Lindquist:

Quite true, Edward. Sadly, it seems many people can't seem to comprehend life beyond their brief lifetime here.

No matter what we do, the Earth will return to its healthy state, whether we still exist or not is of no consequence to the worlds' outcome.

I say, if we can't live here and respect the land, than we don't deserve to live here at all. Let Mother Nature take its course.

Edward Stanulevich IV:

How do you stop Her?

People seem to forget that we are part of nature. Not separate!

If we kill all the bees, we will starve.

We live in cities. We buy our food pre-packaged. Water magically flows from a pipe.

Yet as far removed as we like to pretend we are from nature, it is nothing more than an illusion.

We cannot stop the hurricane, earthquake, blizzard, drought, and tsunami.

We can only stand in fearful amazement at Her awesome power.

We Are Nature!

Pradeep Pk Maheshwari:

It is a sad reflection on how we have evolved. How far removed the mind has become, boxed in by its own super stupidity; just because it was able to learn a few tricks in the realm of physics and chemistry.

Johnny Lindquist

Edward, yes, we are a part of nature, but so long as we can't learn to cooperate with nature, we don't deserve to be here. I had said that we have the same qualities of a virus. That too, is a part of nature, and a crucial one. For when things get out of hand, or start taking over, we have bacteria here to balance things out again.

I think that humans are an intriguing species, and we have gone a long way since our very beginning. I will admit though, I am not very proud of being human. I am very thankful that I have life, but I am part of a species that destroys.

You asked; "How do we stop Her?" I assume you mean nature, and stopping Her from wiping us off the face of the Earth? Join her. Work together.

Everything we take from the land, return. Have a minimal carbon footprint. Make it appear that we were barely even here. For our life is borrowed. Whether there be a God, or whether we are just a series of coincidences, we are only here for a brief time, and as I said, we are borrowing our bodies.

just lost my train of thought lol

Johnny Lindquist:

Pradeep, quite true. Many days, I find myself feeling negative, thinking to myself, our race (human is the only one I chose to see) has let its weaknesses take control of what could be a chance to live a full life, full of greatness and bliss. But instead, we are lost in our greed and blah blah, you get it....

But, back to my near-daily sadness-- on good days, I realize that every generation had the same fear of hopelessness, and near pointlessness, yet some of those who chose to ignore that and go above and beyond are the ones who made history.

The best thing that many can do is smile their way through life, and for those blessed/cursed with a crisp and powerful mind should teach through example.

Edward Stanulevich IV:

Human nature is the only nature we can follow.

Nature destroys species all the time. Long before there were humans, there was extinction. One day, humans will be extinct.

It sounds to me like you are a victim of the Climate Change Guilt Trip.

Climate change killed the dinosaurs. It killed the woolly mammoth. It will kill the polar bears. One day, if we cannot adapt to it, it will kill us.

The Climate cycles. Volcanos explode. We do what we do because we are human.

Ants dig mounds. Beavers build dams. Life is as violent as it is beautiful.

It being short lived, it adds to the beauty.

This too will pass.

Johnny Lindquist:

I like that, the Climate Change Guilt Trip. Perhaps I have fallen victim of that, I agree. But I've always been a little bitter towards the world. I can only hope that we improve our ways.

Pradeep Pk Maheshwari:

They and we and all knowledge that is, will eventually group into wisdom. We shall "see" and go back to the source. There is a direct way and there is the way of destructive instructivity that humans have chosen.

Amir Mourad:

"We do what we do because we are human"

It is part of our humanity, but most of the problems that have been created by man is precisely man has yet to integrate his full humanity. When the whole vast ocean is within his very being, he remains functioning on a superficial level. The problem is that man's consciousness has become cantered around a small dimension of his being, his animal nature. Animal nature is the very language of the body - the body does not know anything else except survival and sex. And if one's whole consciousness is cantered on survival and sex, one is bound to be violent. Animal nature is very beautiful in itself, it has a raw, spontaneous energy - far more natural than the intellect. But whenever any part of one's being is not put into equilibrium with any of the other parts - it is bound to create a disruption in the whole system. Our system is very complex. If the intellect is overwhelming one's intuition, it is going to create a problem. If the intuition is overwhelming one's intellect, it is going to also create a problem. If one's emotion is overwhelming one's intuition or intellect, it is going to create a problem. If one's instinct is not balanced, it is going to create a problem. It is just like if your heart starts becoming under-active or overactive, it will create a disruption for the whole body.

All the parts of our being are part of one whole, interconnected. But because all of our attention has been focused on the external, the inner has been left completely ignored. If every part of one's mind and body were functioning in equilibrium with each other, it would have been impossible to create the kind of problems we have created. Even something like an ego - when it is put into its proper place, supports the whole. All of this that has happened in zen, yoga, and other spiritual sciences about the ego being a problem comes from a certain misunderstanding. The ego is not a problem, it has never been. The problem is an ego which is not balanced within the whole structure of man.

It is not because we are human that we have created a mess on this Earth, it is that we have not yet come to truly flower our full humanity. Otherwise, love would have been inevitable - man would have been naturally peaceful and contented. But amongst all of the creatures on this planet, he is suffering the most. The whole cosmos is in absolute harmony, but man has in a single blink of an eye become isolated, an island onto himself. The river stream has been flowing for centuries, but he keeps trying to swim against the current. And as long as he continues trying to swim against the current, suffering is going to continue. Maybe this suffering is absolutely necessary for him, it simply shows that he has not yet learned from his mistakes, he is still functioning unconsciously. That is why history repeats itself, although it is not history which repeats itself, it is the mind which repeats itself. An element of unconsciousness is something essential in order for man to continue creating the same problems again and again, the cycle of suffering cannot keep on moving without the support of man's unconsciousness.

<u>Edward Stanulevich IV</u>:

Yet I have found that when my survival has been eminently threatened, or I have had a particularly good sex session, I find my Self in the same way as when I have an eminent meditation session. My self lost in the moment, surrendered to my Self.

Does your animal nature have a Buddha nature?

<u>Pradeep Pk Maheshwari</u>:

All intertwined. What you all are speaking about has been part of the Indian tradition in the Occult form of yogic emancipation. The nature already exists but it has to be softly, gradually and definitely pushed towards its own purification and fulfillment. Transformed from the animal to the saint. This is the process ongoing. It is like the making of good wine & liqueur.

First the sapling, then the vine and then the grapes. Followed by pressing/crushing/mauling. Fermentation, Filtering.More time in the cellars. Filtering Tasting.Last touches. Final product.

Going even further and making exquisite liqueur

TOPIC NO 17

Cocksure and Prejudiced

Whatever be our education, we still permit ourselves the luxury of some prejudices and totally unjustifiable generalizations. Some obvious ones are such mistaken assumptions like the one that only women can teach children, or Sikhs are not bright enough or that all south Indians make good secretaries.

Similarly, there are fixed ideas in all the other fraternities too. The police begin with the notion that all are basically criminals. They haven't just yet caught them yet. The lawyer is not very far away from this thought either. The painful point of discord is in the idea that every lawyer thinks that he can get his client off and this is blindly seconded by his client. In general life disaster strikes when mistakenly perceiving ourselves as brilliant we play a tricky one and are sure that no one can see through our machinations.

Mankind is prone to many foolish operations based on their even more stupid cocksure thinking. And when things go wrong, we try to rationalize, find excuses or someone to blame. Whatever the subject, if the matter is such that it can be settled by observation, then take care to observe yourself instead of depending on the hearsay of others. Thinking that we know when we really don't is a fatal mistake that we all make sometime or the other.

Most assumptions are unfortunately not always easy to resolve. Most people have passionate convictions.

The best way to realize your own bias is to pay attention to yourself. If an opinion contrary to your own makes you angry, it is a sure sign that you have really no basis for your own convictions. If somebody maintains that the earth is flat, today, do you get angry? No! You rather pity the person and laugh it off. But in the matters of religion where there is no argument that can be proven either way, the chaos and stupidity results in behaviour and acts that are stupendous and shattering.

Shall we use a little logic and try to become more rational? A little more aware and with the "present"? Be wary of opinions that flatter your self-esteem. Do not believe in the superior excellence of your prejudices.

Edward Stanulevich IV:

"Shall we use a little logic and try to become more rational?"

Religion is a multi-billion dollar industry. So I am going to have to answer 'NO.'

BTW, I do include science under the heading of religion.

I could put politics here too, but religion and science have both contributed to the good of mankind....

Pradeep Pk Maheshwari:

If we stick to the purview of prejudices, would this Q be still out of place? Your response expands the purview of the discussion rather.

Harry Hooker:

Pradeep, thank you so much for instigating so much great conversation.

Human evolution is glacially slow. Sri Aurobindo, observed that "Man is an abnormal who has not found his own normality.....he is not perfect in his own nature like the plant and the animal." For the time being my key to happiness is to keep my intentions high and my expectations low.

we fade into the

bone/cold

heart/iced

entropic void

as the momentum

of the universe

hurls us into

215

the warm embrace

of

Divinity.

hh 5/92 after reading 'The Life Divine'

Pradeep Pk Maheshwari:

Agree. I am a student of the Sri Aurobindo Ashram. I was put in the school at the age of seven. I belong to the first batch of students The Mother took in for Her school from outside of the immediate circle of disciples.

Amir Mourad:

"Shall we use a little logic and try to become more rational?"

One can try to raise one's logic to higher peaks, but without the guiding force of one's intuitive wisdom, one is bound to become entangled in logic. Because logic can be tremendously accurate, but only from a certain limited angle. And reality is such, that it can be expressed from an almost infinite number of angles and positions. That is how logic can even work against itself - it will form one perspective, and then when it comes across another perspective which is the opposite, it thinks the contradiction is a problem. It will work hard to reconcile the opposites - not knowing that there are no opposites in existence and whatever appears as opposite are just complimentary - nothing ever contradicts anything. It just appears to be the case to the intellect, which has its whole language revolving around a linear way of understanding.

Dave Shapiro:

Transcend logic, transcend wisdom, science and belief and transcend Things......that shoreline is awaiting

Harry Hooker:

Hi Dave, "....attain the other shore, to beyond the other shore, having never left."

Hi Amir, this is something that I posted on another topic awhile back concerning the evolution of meta-perspective (true awareness), it never gained any traction on that post and probably will be ignored on this one: Please consider the possibility that human experience can be described to a limited extent as perception and perspective. Perception, of course, is the way that we physically take in data from our environment. Buddha, I think, called them the five skandas. As we develop from infants, these perceptions are formed into a fairly stable framework, which represents an individual, cognitive, ordering of our perceptions. This is perspective.

There is a very simple analogy (thanks to Carl Sagan), which can illuminate perspective. Here goes. Two people are standing on a merry-go-round which has a counter-clockwise motion person 'A' throws a ball directly at person 'B' who is located directly opposite (180 degs.) from him. To 'A' the ball appears to curve to his right. To 'B' it seems to go to the left. However, if we erect a scaffold over the carousel, a stationary observer on it would report that the ball went straight and that 'B' moved away from it. 'A' believes that he is right, as does 'B', but the guy on scaffold believes them both to be wrong. What we have here is three different perspectives. But more importantly what we have established here is a meta-perspective, which can hold AB&C in its hand and look at all at once.

From AB&C's perspective there is right and wrong. There does not seem to be any language for right and wrong in the meta-perspective, no left-right, no good-bad, no nut'n.

So maybe, perspective derives from perception and belief derives from perspective. And maybe meta-perspective derives from silence and stillness. Logic will serve any perspective.

Hi Pradeep, what a lucky guy you are to have been in the presence of the greatest philosopher of the last century. I would like to talk w/ you more about you experience w/ Sri Aurobindo and the Mother.

Namaste, all y'all, H

Edward Stanulevich IV:

Harry, well duh it didn't gain any traction!

It is firmly in the middle ground. IF you want comments on your posts you have to go to an extreme. Also, try to make just a little less sense when you post. And contradict people whenever possible.

Watch:

"Transcend logic, transcend wisdom, science and belief and transcend Things......that shoreline is awaiting "

You will never find the shoreline by transcending things. You must embrace the world to find that this transcendence is in the world. You are part of the world, so is wisdom, science, belief and truth. Without the compass to point the way, and the map to guide you, you will wander at sea without ever awakening to the shore.

See, now that was easy.

So, in summary-

1) Pick an extreme

2) Do not make total sense

3) Contradict someone who does make sense

Pradeep Pk Maheshwari:

Now Edward, you have touched a nerve!

Hi. Harry. The basic part of your post seems too complex. We are simple people and need simple words and analogies. It reminds me of the harrowing times I had in school when the teachers were trying to make me understand the Pythagoras Theorem.

Samar Vijay:

Dear Pradeep.

It is all about attitudes. From the very childhood we are programmed to think negative. Tell me honestly, how often have you all told your child (Child, do this otherwise you will be beaten. If you this you will get a beating") why is our communication never complete without this "nahi to"(otherwise)? Let's have honest thoughts from all the members.

Pradeep Maheshwari:

I can say for sure that this has never happened with my child.

Have you followed my other articles?

This is exactly the awareness about the negativity that I am trying to raise.

Dear Pradeep and Samar,

This is a wonderful thread, a commendable topic on which our forum should do a little brainstorming. Samar says it is all about attitude - I do not think so. The attitude comes later,

Pradeep is talking about 'stereotyping' which is the backbone of Bollywood films -which happen to be what each one of us watches several times a week. Thus we unconsciously start believing in all the canards being spread by the invisible scriptwriters. It is the 'perception' here that holds the key.

Stereotyping is so deeply entrenched in our minds, from our school-days till today also we all keep forwarding Sikh jokes, though many of us like myself are painfully aware of the source. Most of these are 'dumb blonde' jokes stolen from the internet and changed to Santa and Banta pairs.

We even have derogatory epithets applicable to our geographical roots :

Panju for a Panjabi, Mallu for a Malayali, Ghati for a Maratha, and Gujju for a Gujarati.

We are all happy, so this stereotyping will continue till Kingdom come.

About the 'cocksure' and prejudiced or biased, even bigoted part of the essay by PK, this is a new and improved version of the age-old argumentative Indian who comes into full bloom in railway compartments, in newspaper's letters to the editor's column, and worst of them all, in TV channels promoting Big Fights in the name of debating. There is so much cacophony and harshness amongst the participants that cultured folks usually skip these 'foaming-at-the-mouth' debates and switch channels.

Traditionally the middle class mentality pushes every child to be as confident and self-assured as M.S. Dhoni or Tendulkar or Sania Mirza : though the child may at heart be an avatar of M.K. Gandhi. Humility has been crushed under our fast-paced feet in a tearing hurry to reach the top rung in society's endless search for more money, more easy money and money at any cost.

Culture is dying, art is dying, sports are turned into big entertainment circuses that have become a fountain of wealth, and civilization is being crushed out of existence. Wrong attitude, of course, has brought to this sorry pass. The oxymoronic state of affairs is : the materialistic society of West is fed up with its mindless search for money and an easy life, and is coming to India to absorb higher values -whilst Indians are aping the West mindlessly. We seem to be paying doubly for being neither Western nor Eastern in our existence.

Thanks and regards

Max Babi

www.maxbabi.com

Pradeep Maheshwari:

Yes Max.

Then there are the added "roles" we are supposed to be:

The bahu(daughter-in-law), the saas(mother-in-law), the respectful son, the reverent employee, the strict teacher and other things of what is the best way to do things.

For example I am not able to explain to anyone that pasteurised milk, sealed & refrigerated does not require to be boiled like we did 50 years ago and the water for coffee when being used from a filtered source need not be boiled all over again - and the coffee served at 100 C.

With new technology, methods have changed but not the mindsets.

New understandings are not welcome. For example: Ideas that babies should be allowed to cry - the plastic type of feeding bottles are given the same treatment for washing and sterilizing as other utensils and the stainless steel bottles of yore etc etc.

We have a lot of info in the head, we talk about it but when it comes to action it is always the age old customary acts, practices and thoughts that we follow and pass judgments on.

Syed Nabeel Ahmad:

This is so awesome, I have done that in the past, hope not to do it again... here are some of what I have come across and sometimes even believed to some extent :(

Pathans and Sikhs are stupid

Punjabis are paindoo(rustic)

South Indians are very educated, more intelligent then north Indians and more dark skinned then north Indians which to an average north Indian obviously means more ugly

Bengalis are less warlike and to put it bluntly coward

Muslims are braver then Hindus

Whites are good managers

Orientals are studious

Blacks are criminal

Jews are mean

and yes I know every single one is absolutely wrong and its bigoted to think this way and I know I have thought this way once I do's know why I wasn't smart enough to see through these stereotypes.

Topic No 18

Saying thine part

Have you noticed how some people can speak their part only in outbursts of some kind? They would be otherwise nice, sane people going about their lives in a circular routine that they have built around themselves. Yet, under their calm exterior there is always some undercurrent of judgmental thoughts flowing quietly which, keeps them perpetually irritated about something or the other.

I have noticed this in myself when I am driving. The need to focus on whatever others are doing is so strong to avoid collisions because in Delhi one drives by the rule that if there is space one has to go in and fill it up or worse if you have a bigger car, your self-importance gives you the right to go ahead first. This creates a situation where you have to drive with one eye on the rear-view mirror and the other three eyes on the left, front and right. Of course there is also this continuous analysis that is humming inside the brain. And every now and then, the perceived stupidity of the other guy vents itself out in expletives.

So coming back to our original premise, we need to consider the why and why-nots of the situation. The question is why some people speak their part only in anger; and this is not just anger, it is also laced with a heavy dose of indignation. Indignation presupposes that the person has been wronged and has been made to suffer due to the unworthy actions of the other guy. This also presupposes that some sort of judgment has already been passed. So, I can safely say that the person speaking out in hot flashes is not being pragmatic, he has not bothered to listen to both sides of the story and feels so strongly that he has been wronged that there is no space for discussions in the situation. The situation is exacerbated by the person's need to not only prove his point but also teach the other malefactor a lesson even if it has to be drilled into his head. This I suppose is what they call road rage when it happens on the highway.

How we tend to work ourselves into lather for very often nothing is beautifully illustrated by a story I read many years ago. It was titled "Want to borrow a jack?"

A motorist had a puncture somewhere out of town and was appalled to discover that there was no jack in his car. Now at the unearthly hour of 4 in the early morning where would he find the assistance needed and that too in the middle of the countryside? Let's not forget that this story comes from a time when cell phones were not invented. So although his head was brimming with anger against all the people who could have done this to him, he was cool-headed enough to look around. In the distance he noticed a light and decided to walk towards it. Soon it became obvious that he was approaching a farmhouse. This got him thinking. "What if the farmer does not open the door? He must surely be sleeping and will be upset at being disturbed at this hour of the night. But my need leaves me with no option but to knock at his door so to hell with the farmer. The farmer can always say no and that will be that and people are so unhelpful anyway nowadays. Etc, etc, etc." By the time he reached the farmer's door he had already worked out his case against the disturbance he was going to cause. If only the poor city-slicker had any idea that farmers get up rather early and are generally the most helpful kind of people on earth as they are deeply in tune with nature's vagaries. Anyway this motorist knocks on the farmer's door and the farmer opens the door. But before anything could be said the motorist blurts out:" Now are you going to give me the jack or not?"

Why are we in such a hurry to prejudge? Why do we feel superior enough to be judgmental with so much righteousness? The other day I was back in my old school which is an Ashram where the morning hours are for meditation and no other activity is encouraged especially in the meditation area and near it. I was sitting there; it was six in the morning. Just then an old lady comes, sees the latest newspaper daily around nearby, left by another ashramite (resident of the ashram) and asks me to tell her the cricket score. So I pick up the paper and open it. After all if the old lady is more interested in cricket scores and meditation is not her forte, who am I to judge? But before I could do my good karma, an old teacher of mine passes by and immediately scolds me for reading the paper in the meditation area! Boy, I was so amused. It was so much like my childhood when I was being scolded for something or the other, never heard nor given a chance to explain. I left immediately and went to the sea beach nearby to cleanse myself of the indignation that this teacher had injected in my atmosphere.

I can understand the young bursting out but one would expect much more from people who have seen a whole lifetime on this earth. When older people behave in this immature manner I do wonder if they have learnt anything at all; especially from people like senior executives, teachers and those in positions of authority. Our courts would not be so filled with cases and divorces would diminish in numbers. Everyday skirmishes would turn into studious discussions.

Why can't people, even if they have been apparently wronged, keep their cool and state their case without anger? Are they incompetent and hiding their incompetence under the banner of outrageousness? I am reminded of this saying by Isaac Asimov –"Violence is the last refuge of the incompetent." And I will leave it here for you to judge!

Grahame Smith:

Very true my friend. I think many people are scared to speak or post their views for fear off what others might say/feel. I suppose people feel they need to fit in, and do not want to somehow look like they are different from their friends etc.

Pradeep Pk Maheshwari :

Yes. One of the sad parts of human thinking.

Johnny Lindquist:

My first thought to this, is comparing humans to the Earth. On the surface of the Earth, it can be very calm, but then several things can happen, whether it be severe weather, or like humans troubles bursting from the inside out, and earthquake.

Dave Shapiro:

My thought on this boils down to control issues. If you lose control or have none in a situation then the emotions can take over if the intellect isn't strong enough to see the underlying factors.....

Teresa Zappey:

This is so true and to think that this week I experienced every part of your writing at school. I do like to be angry but there seems to be times that it is required and needed to stop some particular thing from happening. After the experience I am like you and have to work very hard to cleanse from it. It took me two days to heal from the anger I experienced on Monday. I want to try much harder to not feel anger because it is very damaging. Love hearing from you.

Teresa

Pk Maheshwari:

If only we could realize how irritating we are and what makes us so; then we would recognize the patterns in others and recognize the underlying arrogance/resistance/need to impose control behind most our actions.

This withdrawal into our self will start making us to see with clarity & be amused rather than angry as we shall see the universal subconscient forces at work.

But people will go on with their asinine attitudes and it is so difficult to not get angry.

Side tracking a bit on this issue:

Crazy Wisdom method of breaking your conditioning.

Lama Thupdhen Thumpa is no ordinary monk.

He regularly asks his disciples to the most unconventional and disgusting acts like asking you to rob neighbors drink dirty water and uses such unexpected techniques to shatter seeker's conditioning and notions of good, bad and virtuous.

Crazy Wisdom is a complete inversion of conventional methods. He says he is not a friendly guru teaching yoga and espousing philosophical texts. Those things are soppy, they may comfort you and make you feel better with yourself but they will not awaken you.

He says his job is to shatter the cocoon of your ego and conditioning so that you wake up to your Buddha nature.

People tend to hold tightly to their patterns and nothing short of jolts will get them out of it.

Dave Shapiro:

Sometimes yes..sometimes no...got to know what you are doing to tread that path...can inflict more harm than good...

Pradeep Pk Maheshwari:

Of course Dave, everything in life is sometimes yes or no. But yes as a generalisation it is not an activity for everybody. That is obvious. For one, in the story here it is being practiced by an enlightened one; two it is being put into action on a "seeker" who has come to him (he did not go looking for him) for enlightenment - so this situation is not general - indeed it is very specific, seen the needs of the aspirant.

Mother Nature has been using this technique from day one in her evolutionary process.

Have you noticed how when cultures and civilisations start to stagnate, conquerors or natural devastations seem to erupt from nowhere?

Molly-coddling never brought in change that matters.

Cea Weaver:

You said somewhere: "Let us say hypothetically, I have some energy and view of the Universe and humanity which could help but this knowledge has also made me see that this energy is precious and should be distributed with care."

What energy, what view please; may I know?

Pradeep Pk Maheshwari:

The energy to make changes. Bring forth change. The knowledge of how and where. The wisdom of understanding even why to initiate any change.

Cea Weaver:

"The wisdom of understanding even why to initiate any change." could you explain why we should initiate change please? I'm not sure if I'm clear on this..

Pradeep Pk Maheshwari:

We are locked in an evolutionary cycle. In the normal course of things the movement is moving in a spiral. After every cycle of the spiral, the earth and humanity grow-up a notch.

Seers are those who have & are able to speed up the process and if they choose can help others.

But mostly what happens, one drop of true knowledge and people start crowing and their first instinct is to start telling the world what to do and showing them the way(sic). They see themselves as carriers of Light and want to show it to the world and secretly hope for recognition by the masses as seers. These people create a lot of damage around them.

Topic No 19

Deliberately Rude.

From those times of the beautiful people when good manners were deliberately studied and cultivated and the populace tried to ape them as far as they could, just to be called gentlemen, we have now reached the other end of the spectrum, where being deliberately rude seems to be "IN". It is not an isolated phenomenon. You can go to any corner of the world and you are confronted with humans who refuse to recognize your presence and if they do, they do it with obvious displeasure with grunts or expletives that would have been considered vulgar or abusive some 30 years ago.

The question is why. Are they doing it deliberately? Are they just awfully lacking in education? Are they making a statement of sorts?

If they are doing it deliberately then where did they see the need of it in the first place? If they are lacking in education, once they are out in the world, they could easily learn from example of others around them but they don't. If they are doing it to make a statement, then of course the question is what is it?

It makes me go back to the generation divide question. Every generation announces itself by doing something shocking to make the elder generation take note of their presence and separate identity. I suppose something of the same order is taking place here. The world now belongs to machines and their operators. The middle class with its basic values and education has been edged out. What can we expect?

A deeper study of some instances will make it very obvious.

1) The Girl at the counter of a store today; her job is specific. She has to take the products that you have decided to buy and placed in your basket, pass them over the electronic bar reader and take the money from you. She has no need to know anything about the product or its price of anything at all. The display counter shows the total. Your job is to hand over the cash. All the education the girl needs to be able to count the cash. Every aspect of the thinking and calculating part is done by the machine. Does she need to talk? Not if she does not want to. Just because you have bought an expensive perfume from her store, does not mean she has to be polite to you!

2) The taxi driver; you wave him down. If he stops (Note the "IF") you get in the car. You give him the address and shut up. When you reach there, if you have the rudimentary education to read the meter, you look at the display and pay with a tip for the favour done to you and quickly get out. Displays of camaraderie and even polite greetings are not in order.

3) I go for lunch in a pretty expensive restaurant which happens to be in a busy part of the town. I finish lunch and wish to linger over a coffee. But the waiter has other ideas. He takes away the plates, removes the tablecloth and brings out a new one, snaps it pat into my face and starts laying down the table again for the next customer. The message was clear.

Things are getting worse. At the petrol pump the trend is toward self service. At the store the passing of money is now limited to swiping cards and if technology has its say, this too will be eventually done from a distance. Deliveries are being made at home. The trend is toward minimum human interaction. Any attempt towards conversation, even the commenting on the weather becomes an infringement of the right to remain aloof. Their privacy and freedom is paramount which includes the right to be stupid and a disturber of the peace. You are allowed only to hear their voice when they are incessantly talking on their cell-phones and forcing you to listen to their inane chatter.

So what do I do?

If the rudeness is more than you can take, stay at home. Use your mobile to order things and limit your outings to five star locations, where for your money they will be polite and even extra-polite and may even tolerate some reasonable amount of your ire.

Edward Stanulevich IV:

I was raised in a culture of "STRANGER DANGER!!! :O"

What this means is that around every corner are inconspicuous looking people who are out to get me, kidnap me, poison me with candy, or perform other heinous acts of violence on my person. This included the Catholic priests.

Now, this climate of "STRANGER DANGER!!! :O" was established with good intentions. With all of the child abductions, murders, molestations, and whatnot in the early '80's, parents were very concerned about the safety of their children. They wanted us to do things in a way that would minimize our risk of making the 10 o'clock news.

Inadvertently, they indoctrinated us with a fear of people we do not know. Oddly, to protect us from these horrible fates, they warned us about the dangers of strangers. Yet most of these crimes were committed by people the children knew. Often the parents knew the perpetrators too.

It has taken me many years of personal work to overcome this fear of strangers. This indoctrination of fear has made it very difficult for me to just walk up to someone I do not know and talk to them. Over the past few years I have made a good deal of progress in liberating myself from this overused indoctrination. I am no longer afraid to talk to people I do not know.

At 29 years old, I no longer worry about being abducted. I know that sounds funny, but programming done in one's youth will affect you as an adult. Even into my early 20's I was not comfortable with people I did not know.

Now I can talk to people I don't know, though I have learned that it is best to do more listening than talking.

Part of the rudeness of my generation stems from this "STRANGER DANGER!!! :O"

Pradeep Pk Maheshwari:

Wonderfully put Edward. I am in agreement with you; most of the way.

In India Hindus have always taught their children to be wary of Muslims and the sadhus(monks) are baby stealers in orange garb and we should not mix with the janitors and anyway the lower castes are untouchable.

I know only of other countries from some of my travels and friends like you, but in India I am noticing this trend of arrogance of being "Somebody". Suddenly people who had nothing and were "nobody"s now have cars to flaunt and wear clean clothes (fashionable jeans & T-shirts)/footwear and sport the latest gadgets. From their personal viewpoints, they have risen and Risen! They may be comparing themselves to their old social circle and in that particular circle they may be of importance but in life it is easy to forget this little point.

The need to be kind to each other is reducing and this shows in the attitudes.

It is "you pay, you get what you want and you go"!

Dave Shapiro:

I live in a wilderness area with only a very few neighbors. The bear, moose and mountains do all the talking around here....It took me 55 years to get here but was well worth the wait....I did my share in helping out humanity and still do occasionally but otherwise...survive how you can and always remember the Dam Law

You can Die

You can Adapt

Or you can Move

Post.Pradeep Pk Maheshwari:

I have always wondered about the psychology behind the actions of people who will (for example) first crib about not having jobs, then if they are able to get one , then crib about the conditions, and then go in for strikes and union activities that are often blackmails. A thought that does come to mind is that there is a definitely some idea in the back of these

240

people's minds that is influenced by either inferiority or superiority complexes.

I wish to focus on the point - why can these people just adapt or move on? They could also die - which would be convenient too.

Edward Stanulevich IV:

I have always been fascinated with the idea of caste/class systems. Here in the USA such things are alive and well. For all of our rhetoric about equality, liberty and the pursuit of happiness, there is a definite gap between the haves and have-nots.

We do have one advantage in this regard in that your class comes from two sources. Your birth conditions and the choices you make. No one is bound by being born poor. Only their mental status keeps them that way. People are born rich and often lose it all due to bad choices. You do have the opportunity to advance yourself on the social scale if you choose to put the work in.

Most people who try to do this make one fundamental mistake, and that is the root cause of our economic crisis (not Wall Street, the Banks, Bush, Obama, Congress, Rosie O'Donnell, or Bigfoot). They live outside of their means. People who are actually rich stay that way by spending less than they have coming in. People who appear to be rich do so by spending more than they have coming in. They do this by going into debt.

We have followed this mentality, which is held by the majority of Americans, that debt is necessary, as a country. We worry about out credit scores, which are used by those who loan us money to decide how bad they want to screw us. It is this obsession with living outside of our means that has put us in this predicament.

Now, lower class people do not have as much to worry about here. They do not have the financial means to be allowed to go as deeply into debt. They are often told that they deserve this or that. The government is more and more making them dependant on government aid. We should be trying to raise them up with education and real help, not hold them down with charity. I am not saying charity is bad, but when you make a person reliant upon you for help, you are not helping them.

The middle class are the ones who bear the brunt of the burden. We have the special ability to go hundreds of thousands of dollars in the hole. We buy cars we cannot afford. We buy houses large enough for a small village. We use credit card to spend money we don't have on stuff we don't need. This is what we are expected to do.

People who are truly rich simply don't do this. They often pay cash for their cars, boats, and planes, whatever. They may have houses suited to house a large village, but, they can actually afford to have them. They do not carry significant balances on their credit cards.

Here, it is more about the habits that you live by than the ones you were born into, that determine your class.

I have known people who were truly well-to-do, and they do not live the way you would expect. They were also not miserable, miserly people, as they are portrayed in popular culture. I have also known many more who seemed to be very well off, but who were swimming in debt that they were struggling to pay.

It is our obsession with debt that has put us in our current weakened state. It is our obsession with debt that is pushing so many middle class people into the lower class.

Pradeep Pk Maheshwari:

This is precisely my understanding too. This is how we understand Americans from this distance. We also see the caste system that has evolved there due to the colour of the skin and country of origin without forgetting the original habitants that were displaced and looked down upon by the coming of the Europeans. So now you have this ruling class and the sea of people who wish to ape the ruling class and be one with them but prefer to remain stuck in their own traditional lives based on the country of their origin.

I have a lot of family in the US. Once they reach there, they tend to forget us as poor country cousins. But they do nothing but make their money in the liberal atmosphere of the US. I have people who have been there since two generations, but personally have made no friends with anyone else of another race.

In the 80s I came twice to USA. It was the time of the Govt trying to cut down on the Dole/social security amount. I was shocked to see the media portraying the President as a monster who was depriving the poor. A woman was being interviewed on the TV and she was complaining that if they reduce the amount, she will not be able to repair her car and then how will she go out to look for a job?

This was the time when in India it took 2 years salary to buy a scooter. And credit was unheard of. If we wanted a loan we touched family and friends and were under severe social pressure to pay it soon.

But then Citibank came and established itself here and brought a bit of the US style here. And the mess and havoc it has done to the system needs to be seen to be believed. They started by giving out credit for cars, credit cards and now everyone has cars, no sense of the rules, totally oblivious that there are other guys out there. The driving licenses are bought and so are the traffic police. We are drowning in rudeness and road rage, fast driving when drunk, bad/unlighted/nonexistent roads etc

Socially we are reaching an explosion point as there is no regulation about making parking space in your own homes so people have built parking spots outside the houses and blocked the roads - quarrels and murders are becoming regular things and new cars get stolen quietly and for this you consider yourself lucky or you might even be stopped by motorcycle gangs and asked to hand over the keys. The police is there only to make money out of it all. So the rich get away. Money rules/ you are judged by it and this has created another good cause for showing off bigger cars.

This is just one of the scenarios.

Dave Shapiro:

He/she who dies with the most toys wins.......and I think the debt is just a symptom of the need to fill up on material things because the emotional and spiritual needs are not being met.....just like many (not all) heavy people eat to compensate for loss of love or affection.....just some passing thoughts on the matter...

Pradeep Pk Maheshwari:

Yes Dave. All we have to ask is why do we need to show off and all the answers will come and stand before us.

Claire Willing:

I absolutely know what you mean Pradeep, however I found that a sunny disposition normally works to bring a smile and even pleasantries from most, albeit only to the best of their abilities, granted. All others that cannot be reached at that moment for whatever reason, I cannot remember as I was Far too busy being happy :)

Pradeep Pk Maheshwari:

I have no problems with the attitude of others. They are welcome to whatever cloak they wish to wear. I ask these questions because one would have thought that after so many thousands of years of learning, the world would be more in tune with the sunny disposition you talk of and know better.

There is an obvious something at play that is helping us destroy everything we have had. We are attacking ourselves and the Mother earth and what else is there?

Claire Willing:

I agree with you again, and feel that now is the time when we can ill afford to note the failings of others in moments like the ones that you speak of. People have lost their way and need help, and the help that I speak of has to come from each one of us in each of our moments with others. I am aware of the problems of our world and do what I can to aid the bigger picture also, but each of our lives exists as a series of moments, it is these moments alone that are the only things we can truly do anything about, as I am sure you already know. ⁂ All is said in love and not opposition dear friend :)

Pradeep Pk Maheshwari:

The fault of others is not the focus. The Q is why is this happening. Until we understand the cause, the solution would not be total.

Claire Willing:

Wow this is an enormous topic, and I feel requires a face to face discussion as my typing is not up to it :) However because that is not possible all I can say is that people have lost themselves. We are so used to being told what to do, how to do it, how not to do it, how to behave how not to behave and so much more. All of this coming not from dear family members but from laws and schools and rules (Nanny state). People's moral judgment is almost nonexistent; they have forgotten how to think for themselves. If the family unit was able to arise to the status that it should have, then I feel that at least would help, however the way that this world is wired at the moment means that more time is spent out of the family unit, because of the need for money, school etc. Over the years this has led to most not even being aware of the importance of family in society, and unfortunately, increasingly the new generations coming through do not know how to have and be the support that they never had within the family unit, for their own up and coming families. This is just one of the reasons that I feel contributes to this problem, there are many others but they are far deeper.

Pradeep Pk Maheshwari:

Yes.

Susan Connors:

Hello PK and friends,

This is an absolutely wonderful discussion. I think that the subject matter is very important to examine...just why are people today so seemingly different than they were 20 or more years ago? Yes, rudeness is rampant. "Please" and "Thank You" seem to no longer be civil requirements in Western culture (which now includes major cities in India as I understand it.)

As far as I can determine, the level or rudeness increases proportionate to the amount of technology we put in our lives and in the lives of children. Cell phones, iPods, blackberries and all of the increasing use of 'texting' make real human interaction seem unnecessary thus I propose an age requirement for the purchase of many of these devices that stunt the development of children's brains, much like alcohol or drugs. Let's say age 18. Let's let young have a chance to develop 'normal' communications skills before technology makes those skills seem unnecessary. Thanks for the chance to include my thoughts.

Topic No 20

Teaching Methodology

The roots of our teaching methodology are way back in the old public schools of England; A system which developed when only the blackboard was the teaching-aid available and of course some books. This method with very little change has been in use and continues to be in use in most of the schools of the world.

In the so called developed countries, the digital technology has taken over and has caused a wide gap between the use of gadgetry in life and the teaching methods in use. The students that are being taught by the teacher (audio) and blackboard (video) method are actually being raised in life on the TV and Computers + pre-programmed products. Their brains are tuned differently.

The time has come to understand that gadgets do a lot of our thinking for us. These products are there to stay so we need to take all this into account and our teaching patterns and program needs to be adapted accordingly.

It all started with the calculator. Sums we could in our head but now we need a calculator. Logarithms are child's play.

Digitally every product has taken out the thinking and mistakes out of our lives. Somebody has done the thinking and programmed it all for us. All we need to do is press buttons.

This is why I suggest using movies — and a lot of them. They take the student INTO the period rather deeply and leave a mark on the personality. And that is all that is needed to live life eventually.

As an example I would like to point out the change in the use of the camera. In the 60s we needed to know all about shutter speeds and apertures and film sensitivity and different lenses etc. Today the camera just needs to be clicked. All we need to have is an eye for framing the picture. This is the talent that needs to be nurtured. The rest is a waste of time. If there is keenness in the student, there is a lot of stuff available and he would know where to find what is what; all he needs is to be aimed in the right direction by his teacher.

ON TEACHING History -from a discussion on Facebook

Dave Shapiro:

Congrats to the State of Texas School Book Board and their ability to re-write history to meet the standards of the religious right. California is in the process of making sure none of your books get into their state and it is just a matter of time before the ACLU, NAACP and School Boards around the country refuse to buy into your ignorance and religious bigotry...

Edward Stanulevich IV:

LOL!!! Y'all think anything written in a history book is true?

It is nothing but opinion. The opinion of some old white dude.

Half of history is lies. The other half is opinion.

Dave Shapiro:

Edward: most are aware that history is written by the victors, the academics or the publisher's brother. Yes it is often opinion and never contains all the facts. But, it does give us some ideas about how we got here and now with the internet we can dig deeper into any subject for more in-depth info.....which will probably be biased in another direction...

Pradeep Pk Maheshwari:

Don't forget the need to praise the ruler/winner (in battle). The words of the historian could mean life/death and/or an estate to live upon/on. So a lot of the history as written is also poetry and imagination in full swing.

History books should be removed from our schools and videos/movies put into the curriculum (another instance of imagination at work).

Dave Shapiro:

Like the video idea but do they have some of those with pics of real dinosaurs, gladiators and the war of 1812? Or do you see all printed material eventually going digital with no more need for books???

Pradeep Pk Maheshwari:

Let's not forget the movies already existing. Just use them. All we need to do is make a selection and make the students watch them - even perhaps along with their families; More enjoyable, more retention and educative in many ways. Example: Gone with the wind has much to teach; At least the gentler behaviour patterns. Ryan's Daughter is an experience. 55 days in Peking is eye-opening. El Cid is memorable. Ten Commandments will do more good than 1000 hrs of the priest's babble. Then My Fair Lady will teach more about refined language and behaviour than any finishing school.

Ivanhoe and The count of Monte Cristo will create interests in the classics, even recent ones like Elizabeth teach more history than books.

There are thousands of very good movies out there.

You would have seen Living desert? And recently the ones like Jurassic Park etc.

Dave Shapiro: Now I understand....great idea.....

So let's imagine a classroom 50 years from now.....kids could learn from home on a two way video server.....books would probably become less used.....the TV, phone and Computers will be integrated into one screen on the wall with voice commands and 3-d graphics. Cell phones will be implanted in or near the ear and ………

Pradeep Pk Maheshwari:

 Now you are painting a terrible picture.

I just want to see movies become part of the curriculum. Like:

CIVIL WAR: Basic details like: when, why and how in one para or so and then name of movies to see like assignments: Gone with the Wind etc etc.

All the other things like behaviour etc the kids imbibe without knowing - subconsciously; without any ego/personality clash with the teacher.

Steve Lochmueller:

The inherent problem with the type of teaching that is being described here is quite simply that we would not produce proper working machines for the establishment. Those of us that toil for the betterment of the economy are merely viewed as assets for the corporation. Our ability to think and reason is not considered to be necessary. There are different levels of education designed to produce the proper machines for the designated functions required. Capitalism is never going to allow individuals to become educated beyond their intended function; this is why the U.S. education system has been in decline for years. The machine must never know its a machine

Pradeep Pk Maheshwari:

 Goodness that makes my idea a non-starter. So much for trying to think beyond borders.

Ana Pyxis:

 And what about the bad ones, in historic terms, like Alexander the Great? I don't see much difference in books vs movies, if anything I prefer books. It's just more satisfactory to me imagining all the people, events, scenery, and seeing a movie afterwards is nice to compare, but, to me books come first. Would be nice if kids would like both, reading and watching, but reading, sadly, seems to be disappearing. It's just not in.

Pradeep Pk Maheshwari:

What's the point in passing judgments such as good or bad Ana? They were what they were under the compulsions and possibilities and understanding of the times. Wars have always destroyed but also helped renew and expand cultures. More to the point is the Q of books or films: The idea is aimed at the larger & more average population. Reading can be too intellectual. The plan to use movies is behind the concept of taking them "There". It has a deeper impact. The visuals are terribly important. And let's them not brush them lightly under the carpet. The effort and creativity that goes into each movie is stupendous.

Would you say that Ben Hur and the Ten Commandments are worthless/cheap shows and that nothing is to be gained by watching them?

Dave Shapiro:

I remember both these movies more clearly than any book I ever read as a child other than maybe Mad Magazine....

Ooi Kok Wan:
I learn a bit of Taoism through comics since primary school... does it make any different?..."

I learn the meaning of compassion from watching "National Geography".. when I see how human action effect mother nature... somehow I got the dream to be a terrorist.. >.<"

<u>Kim McMenamin</u>:

 Curiosity is something that does not need to be taught, it needs to be directed. Not every student's interest is going to be piqued by the same manner of delivering the message. Try everything and keep what works.

<u>Pradeep Pk Maheshwari</u>:

 Agree. But the educationists refuse to see this simple point.

<u>Pradeep Pk Maheshwari</u>:

 Any audiovisual method is Okay as long it is not being "TAUGHT". There is an inherent resistance to being taught. Movies, comics and such make us believe we have discovered something for ourselves. It is far more in tune with   our   inner   selves.
My entire learning is based on comics and films. Reading came long after and that too because I had already got interested in the basic stories. The thirst for more made me go to books.

Susan Connors:

One of the problems I have is that your proposal further removes reading from teaching. While I agree that people learn differently (e.g, hearing/seeing or reading/writing) and that it is true that gadgetry has contributed to the way children now *expect* to receive information, I am going to be one of those who continues to fight to keep kids reading as a significant part of their learning.

My partner sees the results of insufficient reading and writing education in lower grades as he teaches high school. Most of them hate reading (actually are semi-literate only), don't know how to write a complete thought, cannot spell, can't do basic math, etc. This is abysmal and has taken the US from #1 in education to #29 in education in the world in about 30 years. (There is also the aspect of lack of respect for adults and/or authority that is very disturbing.)

As it is, some teachers do play movies in their classes and this has not proved to be effective as education. Films ultimately become a classroom babysitter just as TV is at home, even when the subject matter contains correct historical references. Kids tune out quickly to anything.

Pradeep Maheshwari:

I must admit that films can only give glimpses into certain facets of life. Nothing can compare to the focused info in a book.

But yes, there has to be first a spirit of seeking. And this I agree is not being ingrained.

PK:

- I often wonder of how much of our life is "Considered Gestures" rather than real living?

- What is real living?

- Good question. But does this sound reasonable: True to one's own soul?

Catriona Macleod:

Hi Pradeep, I listened to a radio program a few years ago about a psychologist who went round schools working with children with special needs in learning whom the schools had rejected as uneducatable. She eventually founded her own school taking in these kids. She found the majority of them to be exceptionally bright, with very high IQ's just unable to fit into mainstream.

She also said most of the education kids get at school is a complete waste of time and that once they know the basics..3 R's... they're set for life. All that then remains is that they are given the opportunity to pursue their own interests. So it's pretty simple really.

She helped thousands.......I'm sorry I don't remember her name but she was based in London. I thought you might be interested.

Topic No 21

Fear of rejection

The way I would approach this subject is by analyzing the two words first. Why are we afraid at all? It is the opposite of courage. So you have had the gumption to attempt something; this is very fine; rather you should be proud to have stepped outside the comfort zone. And if you are afraid, then it means that a wish is attached to the action. Is that true?

Life comes in two hues; Black and white and hundreds of shades in between and then there all the colours and millions of combinations and shades of these colours. Did you really expect that life would be one roller coaster ride where all you have to do is wish and your fairy Godmother would make it come true? This is awfully unrealistic and terribly childish.

Let us examine this subject from a realistic point of view with some not so hypothetical instances to illustrate the point. A highly learned teacher with a lot of experience goes to a school for a job for which he is more than qualified. But the job goes to a younger lady. The poor man can take this as a rejection and also as a confirmation of the moving ahead of the wheel of life. In the game of life and the truth behind this incident, there is the fact that the school is a business. The administration wants younger people to work hard and daylong. Then as children are involved, there is this notion that ladies are kinder and softer in their approaches; which may or not be true but it is real fact that we have to live with.

Then as the teacher needed is for classes well below the qualifications offered by the learned teacher, he is not really required. So the great expert is not given the job. Does this qualify as rejection? No, not at all.

It is just the quirks of life at play. There are more than a couple of factors at play in life. The more qualified teacher should not take this personally and not bring his vanity into play. Rather, he should take this as an eye-opener and look for greener pastures and I would add improve himself for a greater destiny.

Lately a little downturn in the economy has prompted many companies to downsize with many people suddenly finding them selves back to square one. They can't take this personally. It is definitely depressing and the future with all the commitments at stake is in jeopardy; at least as was visualized. But then life does not move in a straight line. The fear if any is surely from the fact that certain financial commitments had been put into place and now the lack of an income would destabilize the entire thing. In all simplicity I presume to ask, did you plan for not having a job?

Let us say you bought a car on loan which you had planned to pay for as you went along and now this retrenchment falls like a block of bricks on your head. The fear is that either you will have to return the car and lose all the money already paid for or pay for it from your reserves if any. The running of the car is also an expensive proposition. Also here is the image problem. What will everyone think? Now let us speak in realistic terms: Your plans for your life were unrealistic. You were spending money which you had not. You were aiming for things that were not yours as yet by right. And the fear of being ridiculed is purely vanity at work.

There is additionally a positive side to fear. If we are not comfortable with things as they are, we strive to change. We make efforts to upgrade our abilities and think creatively and explore many other possibilities which we would have not done otherwise. This results in an educative process which benefits us greatly and will stand by us more than anything else in the world in times of crisis.

In relationships "Fear" takes a slightly different colouring although the shapes being coloured are the same. Our vanity asks us to modulate our behaviour and we then present ourselves to the liking of others and their appreciation. In our zeal to impress we present a very false persona. We are being untrue; to ourselves and to the other. Sooner or later, the other person will see thru the machinations. And if the other is a wizened, experienced person, he will see it immediately. This is manipulation which can never have a good ending; we bluff, huff and puff and blow our own house down. If we get hurt in the process, we alone are totally to blame. In relationships, if we were truer, honest and candid, we would not pose or compromise our feelings at every step. We would have the courage to say NO when we want to and only YES when we really mean it. We would also pay attention and listen to the other, especially when the other is trying to say NO.

In the final analysis there is nothing to fear but to strive is. You are you and you should take yourself positively but with a pinch of salt. The anxieties and pain come from the 'wants" we impose on ourselves with finicky attitudes so all we need to do is de-complicate our lives.

Priya sharma:

Hello Pradeep, Nice article and very true. Give courage not to fear. Sometimes when you get ditched by your beloved one so deeply this fear comes in your heart and soul and remains there for forever.

Fear of fake relations

Fear of dishonesty etc.

PK:

Yes Priya.

In my own life, one young lady gave me such a jolt that I could not bear for any relationship of any kind for many years.

I was not though afraid. I just got so put off that I lost interest in humans.

Today when I look at it after more than 30 years, I see that it still has a lot of influence on my Psyche.

Priya:

Hi Pradeep,

Same is my case.

My husband bilked me and my kid in such a bad way that today we are in same condition. With broken heart and trust, life looks like a pain; but anyhow I have to be strong for my kid.

PK:

Ah yes when there is a kid, the equation is different.

I soon learnt that human relationships are need based. Even the so called divine relationships have a selfish core to them.

Our loves are based on judgments that we pass on each other all the time and our attitudes therefore can change from one day to another. Unconditional love is a concept and should be a possibility but humans are not designed that way.

When we stick to each other, there is rarely ever a 100% giving or taking. We are together and sometimes stuck in relationships as we have no options due to natural, social, legal or other compulsions or just because we have or don't (see) any other options.

The fear of rejection finally faded away when I realised that I was barking up the wrong tree worrying about and wondering if I would be liked/accepted or not. Once I learnt to be happy with my own self, this fear went into oblivion.

But I also found that, this is possible only when we are honest, kind & committed. Keeping our word, being forgiving, speaking and acting only because we mean it and living simple uncomplicated lives both in thought and in action is important.

The others will live their lives; we should live ours. If a common friendly platforms can be found, so much the better....otherwise.....it is a big enough world for all of us.

Ana Pyxis :

" Once I learnt to be happy with my own self, this fear went into oblivion.

But I also found that, this is possible only when we are honest, kind & committed. Keeping our word, being forgiving, speaking and acting only because we mean it and living simple uncomplicated lives both in thought and in action is important.

The others will live their lives; we should live ours. If a common friendly platforms can be found, so much the better....otherwise.....it is a big enough world for all of us.:"

Very nice Pradeep. Knowing myself, trusting my heart and my common sense is the most important, first step. Then I'm able to react in an honest and compassionate manner to others as well.

I came across this "Gestalt prayer" the other day:

"I do my thing and you do your thing.

I am not in this world to live up to your expectations,

And you are not in this world to live up to mine.

You are you, and I am I, and if by chance we find each other, it's beautiful.

If not, it can't be helped."

Amir Mourad:

Ana, "Knowing myself" - What do you mean by this?

Ana Pyxis:

Knowing myself means I am what I perceive of myself, what I know (now) to be right and true for me, what I can and can't, what I want and seek, what made and makes me who I am, what influences me, makes me sad or happy, knowing my virtues and flaws, my possibilities and limits. I would say that knowing my (ego) self is necessary to, hopefully, one day, know my true self.

....

Ana Pyxis:

Nicely put Pradeep. The fear of rejection, or any fear that prevents me to stand up for myself, speak my mind, be who I really am and not what I think others would expect from me, is devastating in the long run, so let me put it this way - Thank God I found Zen! :D It did help me get rid of fear, actually it's a process, but I think it's going well so far.

Dave Shapiro: When you can say that about death then you

have won this battle...

Ana Pyxis: As strange as it may seem that is the least of my

265

fears, I'm still more afraid of what life may bring.

Topic No 22

No Time for Humouring

From the point-of-view of an anthropologist, when historians in the future will be speaking about the "AGE" we are passing thru, how do you think we shall be seen & remembered? As a social people what we have achieved as our most important facet? Let us see, is it our constant connectivity with each other, our spiritual search or stress & depression?

I was wondering where this humanity was heading yesterday after an altercation with another driver who blocked my way and kept on asking me to go on the wrong side to give him way. I refused and as a matter of principle just stopped my car and waited for him to correctly go back to his side of the road. He did but did not forget to launch a few abuses at my back. Then I came back home and tired and fatigued by driving in the noisy, dusty & unrelenting 42 deg C heat of Delhi and all and asked my wife to sit down with me and share a cup of coffee. What I got was a retort that – "can't you see I am busy?"

Then the other day I was discussing a point with a friend and she asked this poignant question – "I am tired of everyone rushing around, filling their days with solo activities and then trying to stay in touch using the various medias with no in-person contact. I would like to see my friends make an effort to connect with me in the flesh. I would consider it a joy to make em' a cup of coffee and engage them in conversation or small talk, whichever they choose. I can't understand why they won't come out and play?"

This is when the penny dropped. All these gadgets that help us communicate and run our lives from a distance have done us the disservice of permitting us to undertake more than we have time for and still be able to manage things somehow. In the process we just have no time for anything else. And non-essential things like chatting up a friend or lending an ear to somebody is the first thing that goes off our list. Everything is being reduced to straight and simple functional practicality. If close relationships like marriages are seeing this trend then what is there left to say of other more casual relationships?

The situation has reached such an impasse that our attitudes have brought to the fore our self-centeredness and has resulted in our own isolation. At any given time we are so mentally stretched that we are easily irritated and curtness is becoming a normal feature.

It is easy to understand why it is so attractive to keep in touch through Medias like Face book. I must add I love the interaction on Face book because it is direct, to the point and there is no waste of time. Then there is also the complete lack of worry about keeping up appearances. Even in places like shopping malls and stores or while travelling there is a distinct sourness to be seen. 20-30 years ago people were happy to be chatted up and were happy to share a paper or a cup of tea with you. Now if you try they look at you as if you are up to some unpardonable sin. Anyway if they do respond, they will leave you staring at the space above their head, the moment their mobile phone rings.

I request people who visit me to shut off their phones, especially if it is a business or commercial visit; otherwise I ask them to go out and finish their conversation. After that I make it clear that if they are going to ask for my time, they are welcome but if they will continue to allow us to be disturbed by the mobile then I am sorry I am not available and ask them to politely leave. I am definitely not interested in a triangular relationship in which the mobile phone has priority.

Leave alone the world at large, we do not have time to listen to our children, do things at their pace or just enjoy their company. Now this is criminal. I see most mothers who bring their toddlers/young ones in the park here in the evening spending their time talking on their phones while the child fends for itself. Now what kind of mothering is this?

Take any situation, any relationship; there is simply no time or inclination to humour anybody. There is no patience and of course no need is ever felt. I remember once when I was just about 19 or 20 years old, when I was with one of my father's friends, he said hullo to some elderly friend of his and asked "how are you?" The other person told him in detail how he was. Regaling with all the latest news, visits to doctors and all. I was astonished to see that my father's friend never showed any irritation or impatience and very pleasantly heard him through. Now here was a lesson to take note of.

This is what makes me conclude that we shall be remembered as a dismembered society where our selfishness and preoccupation with "self" has left no place for any kind of humouring; not even in the least bit.

No wonder now we have computers, radios and phone that wish us good morning and a mechanical dog comes to wake us up in the morning. The worst is that the coffee too comes from a machine with no smile or hug to go along with it.

Like no car zones, perhaps we should have no phone zones or/and no electricity days.....

Catriona Macleod:

Re: No time for humouring

Totally true! It isn't healthy. Not only that it isn't real! Pure escapism.....

Robin Roberts:

I do agree with your observation Pradeep. I don't understand when it became necessary to be available to everyone 24/7. I came up with my own rules and it helped me to regain a bit of my sanity. If I am with another, I simply do not answer the phone, that is what voice mail is for. I absolutely will not answer or talk on the phone while driving….driving is not down-time, it is a major responsibility with life or death consequences and deserves our full attention. I enjoy FB, but I limit the time I spend here. If company comes over and the TV is on, the TV gets turned off immediately, the phone is ignored. I no longer think I'm going to miss something, if I do, so what? I can tell you the world doesn't end, and who needs all the excess mental clutter all the time.

I have found this works not only well for me, but has improved my relationships. I know I'm going to get creamed for posting this, but others should try it, they might just like it.

Jane Higgins:

You are totally right PK, they are going to the leader's of the World one day, and need to have been taught the old timey way of being good, kind and nice to people, especially the older people.

Janelle Portelli:

Um sadly the kind I see all too often, until I can be b sure that my mobile will not outweigh the evening with my child I'm not even thinking of having any...that's just me though, in this age its becoming more accepted that its the way it is, but I have found that children sometimes are the last thing that parents are concerned about, and these children get into the middle of things they have no idea about.... (I'm not judging anyone, I'm not a mom yet, not sure if I'll get the chance but I'm a qualified youth worker when I work), and that they don't give much time. When the kids are being cared for, they are mostly teens and I used to get them to help... not letting kids fend for themselves. Are not parents meant to be examples and role models..... I know that's idealistic but I hear you Pradeep!!!!

Re: No time for humoring

Rita Maker

"LEISURE"

What is this life if, full of care,

We have no time to stand and stare.

No time to stand beneath the boughs

And stare as long as sheep or cows.

271

No time to see, when woods we pass,

Where squirrels hide their nuts in grass.

No time to see, in broad daylight,

Streams full of stars, like skies at night.

No time to turn at Beauty's glance,

And watch her feet, how they can dance.

No time to wait till her mouth can

Enrich that smile her eyes began.

A poor life this if, full of care,

We have no time to stand and stare.

By Wm. Henry Davies.

Comment by <u>Richard Penney</u>

You make very succinct points! I have noticed that people have stopped having conversations. Our life styles are too busy to be connected with others. I see the "soccer moms" and every one rushing toward their fate with no heed of the passage of chances to connect in a meaningful manner. The only thing which matters in the final accounting is how we treat and are treated by others. Emotions are the reason for remaining on the wheel of 84.

- -

Contact: gururdeva@yahoo.com

phone India(0091) – 011 41730043

On Facebook look me up under PRADEEP PK MAHESHWARI & my group & page under the name: Academy of Behavioral Therapy

Person to person counseling and workshops offered.

Feel free to contact me anytime between 3-6pm

About the author:

Professional Manager, with 40 years experience in managing people and doing business in India & internationally. Industrial family background. Well travelled in India and abroad - specially in the French belt in Europe & well educated in both Indian and European classical

273

streams, speaking English, French and Hindi . With background of applied psychology and physics, teaching & soft-skills training. Practitioner of Holistic medicine. Qualified Interior Designer (USA). Landscaping in oils and photography are my hobby. Experienced in Design and Development – consumer goods. Very well versed in Indian cultural biases, history and commercial attitudes. Published author.

Student of Sri Aurobindo Ashram, Pondicherry.

Contact: phone: +91-11-41730043,

Facebook: Pradeep PK Maheshwari.

274